Cop

Copyright © 20.. ...nson

All rights reserved.

Cover design by Elliot Webb / AbleArk.com
Book design by AbleArk LLC

This book is a work of non-fiction. Names, characters, places, and incidents either are products of the author's imagination or are used fictitiously. Any resemblance to actual persons, living or dead, events, or locales is entirely coincidental.

By purchasing this book you are assuming that all risk from the instructions offered within this book are your own responsibility. And that I cannot be held personally responsible for any loss, damage, expense, or injury sustained to your personal property, or your person when undertaking any of the steps outlined in this book. It is all assumed at your own risk and common sense.

Gary Johnson
howtoinstalllaminateflooring@gmail.com

First Printing: Nov 2013
AbleArk LLC

Contents

Introduction

About Me:

My name is Gary Johnson, I'm 36, and have been working in and around laminate flooring for the last ten years or so. Not only installing, but also selling laminate flooring as a sales specialist in a major hardware company. So I've heard all the most common questions on both sides of the fence, which I'll share with you throughout this book to help you on your way. But most of all I will take you with me from start to finish, and hopefully the outcome will be a finished laminate flooring installation that you can be very proud of.

I want this guide to empower you with the confidence to install your own laminate flooring. I wrote, "How to Install Laminate Flooring" for regular DIY'ers, weekend warriors, budget conscious families, and even new contractors looking to get a quick idea on how to do it yourself. Why pay hundreds or even thousands of dollars to have someone come to your house and do it for you? I guarantee if you took two minutes to watch how they do it, you will be kicking yourself that you didn't try it yourself. And remember, each square foot that installer lays down, is usually costing you at least $2-$5 for the labor alone. This book costs you less than paying an installer for a few square foot of space. And can empower you to save thousands by doing it yourselves!

This guide-book can be used as a reference, or down at your side while you install your laminate flooring. I wanted to keep it short and to the point and not just filled with all the filler content, history of laminate, and all the yaddi yaddi yadda some of the other guides include. I want this guide to help you each step of the way after you decide that it's laminate flooring you want to install in the first place. I will cover tips and tricks I use when installing floors. I'll also cover common questions I get from customers when I'm on the sales floor. And then we will look at what the pro contractors do to make it even easier to install this type of product.

If I've done my job right in this book, by the end of it you will have not only purchased the laminate flooring, measured your rooms, and got the correct tools. But you will also know exactly what to do to install the flooring and then take care of it when it's completed. And as many of you may already have laminate flooring on your floors. I'll cover some problems and issues you could be finding from faulty installs, or from the laminate flooring just showing its age.

Thank you for purchasing my guide!

Let's get this thing started!

Gary Johnson.

What This Guide Will Teach You

Important Subfloor Information:

Don't ignore this important step in the process! Your subfloor is the foundation of your laminate flooring install, and cannot be overlooked. I'll give you some information and advice to help you build a great flooring installation from a solid starting base.

Product Selection:

How to gauge which laminate flooring to purchase in the first place. Along with Brands, Styles, and other important information you need to know before buying your laminate flooring.

Tools For The Job:

What tools will you be needing to get the job done right? It's all covered in this section along with some money-saving pro tips, that most first-time installers do not know.

Room Layout:

How to plan, layout, and then measure your room. This section of the guide will put you on the right path to buying and figuring out just how much laminate flooring you need.

Design Ideas:

This section covers a few design ideas that won't cost you much extra. But it will make your new laminate flooring look like a million dollars when it's completed! Wanna turn your visitors heads when they enter your room? Then this is the section for you.

The Installation:

The nitty-gritty of this guide offers you a step-by-step view of the entire installation process. It uses real pictures along with computer images of the steps you need to take to install your own flooring. It does not matter if you are a first time installer, or if you own your own laminate installation business. There is something in here for every level. Let me take you by the hand as we cover everything you need to know, from prepping, all the way to laying that last plank. You may also enjoy Math Haters Unite for some really cool measuring shortcuts.

After The Install:

I don't just leave you hanging after the install! This section covers cleaning up using the right cleaners. And, we also go over protecting your laminate flooring for the foreseeable future.

Doctor Laminate:

Using my installation experience to cover what you should do to fix any issues with your laminate flooring. I cover dents and scratches, lifting floors, and the dreaded section on replacing a plank in the middle of the floor. But, as always I offer quick and simple ways to do each one, which can really save you a lot of time, money, and research.

Important Subfloor Information

One of the many pitfalls of a good laminate flooring install could be the actual subfloor you lay it down on! I've met many customers who put a lot of research into the flooring, but missed some very basic subfloor information that either stopped them in their tracks, or caused a ton of problems after! So my first step is to quickly run over some important subfloor rules, so you can start to build on a solid foundation.

Sections covered in this chapter are:
o   The Subfloor

The Subfloor

One of the most overlooked aspects of installing a laminate flooring could be your subfloor. In an ideal world your subfloor will be completely flat, clean, durable, and ready and waiting to be buried under the laminate flooring. However, here are a few things to look out for when checking the condition of your subfloor.

Subflooring by T(h)ed Ferringer

- Before you start to prep your subfloor, you may want to take a look at the laminates manufacturers instructions to see what they recommend under their flooring. -

As you are aware, because of the floating aspect of laminate flooring it can be installed over either a wooden or concrete subfloor, and on all grade levels. Now depending on what one you have, both can raise different issues that may hinder your laminate flooring installation process. Or worse still, it may cause big problems down the road.

The first thing you want to check on the subfloor is obviously its condition. And this simply means to make a quick inspection with your own eyes before you do anything else. Most of the time you will either notice something that sets off alarm bells, or you might get lucky and not really see anything that makes you think it's a bad subfloor. So let's dig a little deeper and learn some of the requirements that good subfloors should have.

Level Requirements:
- The subfloor slope in a 6' span should not exceed 1".
- The flatness of your subfloor must not exceed 3/16" over a 10' radius between two high points and the low point.
- If you are using a 3' straight-edge, the flatness requirement is 1/16".

Traditional Method:
You can use a 3' level or straight edge ruler with a measuring tape to gauge the flatness and the slope of the subfloor. To check the flatness, just move the level around the room making sure everything is as level as

possible. If you do find an area of space between the level and the subfloor, take your measuring tape and measure from the bottom of the level to the bottom of the dip in the subfloor. If this gap exceeds 1/16", you will need to make a mark on the subfloor so that you can come back when you are done to fill in the void. Repeat this step over the entire subfloor, making notes and marks on the areas that will need to be filled in or skim-coated later.

Tight String & Nail Method(Old-School):

Another way to get an idea on how level your subfloor is, but not as accurate, is to find the center of the room and mark a small cross. Now grab a nail, and either a chalk line or piece of string and nail it into the middle of the room, you don't have to go all the way down with the nail, but just enough to secure the string. Next, walk out about 10 feet and pull as tight as you can on the string at ground level, then either nail this end into the subfloor or have someone hold it tight against the floor.

What this technique does is show you any dips or high spots under the tight string represented by a space between the subfloor and the bottom of the string(pictured below). If you find a spot larger than 3/16", mark it on the subfloor with a pen. Now just go in a big 10' circle around the room stopping every 6 to

10 inches marking all the dips or rises.

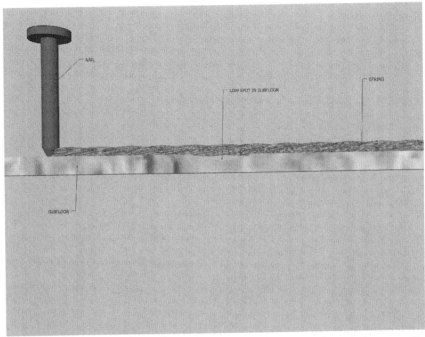

String level test. Basic, but still works pretty well.

Next Step - Fill the Voids or Sand the Peaks:

After you compete a full 10' circle using the string or level method, you will hopefully have a fully flat subfloor. Needless to say some of you will have a few marks on your subfloor that represent either a low area or a high-spot, but fear not, as this is pretty simple to correct.

In most cases you will probably be up against a low spot, and the best thing to use here is a Portland Cement, latex based leveling compound, which can be found at most local hardware stores. You want to mix the compound to the manufacturers recommended instructions, and then just flat trowel over the flat spot to make it even with the rest of the subfloor. You can check it is done correctly by using your level or straight edge before moving on to the next mark. If it seems to be corrected, then just let it dry completely before you even attempt to install the flooring.

If you find a rise in the subfloor, you will probably be needing a sander to knock it down level with the rest of the subfloor. But if you don't own a sander, you can always rent them for pretty cheap at the local tool rental place. I've heard of people using sandpaper! But, that just seems like a lot of work and something that would be better performed with the correct tools. After all, this is the first step and we want to do it right. Remember once you start sanding to keep on checking the level because we do not want to go too far and create a low spot.

Always remember to clean up the mess after you are done!

Check For Moisture:

You must always check the moisture of a concrete subfloor, and even a wood subfloor that is sitting over a crawl space. Moisture test kits are available at your local hardware stores for purchase that will give you readings on the moisture content, which you can then compare with the manufacturers guidelines to make sure it is at an acceptable level.

Basic Moisture Test:

A little method I used when a moisture kit was not available(old school), was to use a 2'x2' poly sheet and some duct tape. I would then secure all side of the poly sheet down with the duct tape making sure air could not get under the sheet. I would then leave it about 24 to 48 hours before I came back to check it. As soon as you peel up the poly sheet it will either be bone dry, saturated with moisture, or may be a little discolored? I've seen puddles at times on concrete subfloors, which is a sure sign that this would not be a good choice for laminate flooring until the moisture issue is dealt with. And of course a bone dry test is a great sign that this is an acceptable subfloor, and pretty much means you can move on to the next step.

If you do notice a discoloration that is neither dry or soaking wet, then to be safe you should still get a proper moisture tester, just to make sure everything is 110% covered under the laminate flooring warranties.

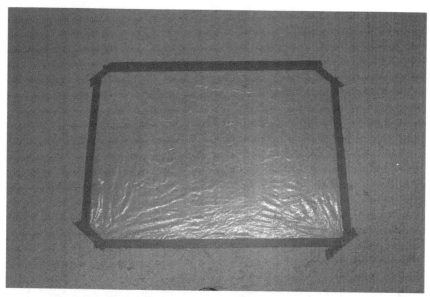

2x2 poly moisture test on concrete subfloor.

We already covered some critical subfloor issues that could hamper your installation progress. But I also wanted to include this quick list of subfloor information, just so you are aware of the other subfloor do's and don'ts.

Subfloor Requirements List:

Never use laminate flooring in rooms with floor drains or sump pumps

Laminate flooring can be installed over sheet vinyl, linoleum, and VCT tiles, as long as they are in good condition. You must also make sure that if you do have this type of flooring currently down, that it is only one layer thick. Too many layers will actually work against the laminate flooring, and eventually destroy the seams because of the excessive flexibility.

You can also install laminate over radiant heat matting, but you should not exceed 84 degrees. Some manufacturers also prefer that you do not fluctuate the temperature of the in-floor heating over a certain range, and in a specific period of time. So if you do choose to go with radiant in-floor heating, please check with the company what their terms are for doing so.

Concrete:
- Concrete must cure for at least 60 days before an install.
- Must remove any current wooden flooring on concrete subfloor before the install.
- Must always use a 6mil polyethylene film to form a moisture barrier under laminate(even if flooring comes with a pre-attached padding - and even if installing over existing sheet vinyl or VCT).

Wood:
- Must use 6mil polyethylene on wooden subfloor over a crawl space.
- Nail or screw into subfloor to stop any squeaks.
- Always check local building codes to meet

thickness requirements.
- ○ Always remove any carpet padding and tack strips from the subfloor.

Funny side-note:

I had a customer complain that his laminate flooring was too spongy when walking on it. Here is basically how the entire conversation played out.

Customer: "It feels like a trampoline sometimes!"

Me: Confused I asked, "Who installed it?"

Customer: "I did. Thought it looked really easy!"

Me: "What did you use for a padding?"

Customer: "Oh, well I had to take up my carpet before I installed the laminate, and I noticed that the padding looked in great condition. So I used that under my laminate flooring, to save money on extra padding!"

Me(in disbelief): "Well, that might be the cause of the spongy feeling under the laminate!"

Customer: "Ya, probably not a good idea now, but seemed great at the time? You think it will be okay?"

Me: "Ummmmm?"

This goes to show you how far ahead you are in your own laminate flooring journey! ;-)

What will happen to that customers floor? Well, because of the constant flexing in the laminate with a thicker carpet padding underneath, it will eventually tear the seams apart, or even the planks depending on how thick the product was that he purchased. But not good, any way you look at it!

Product Selection

In recent years you may have had very few choices on what laminate flooring to purchase. Now however with the popularity of this flooring growing by the day, more and more companies have entered the laminate flooring market with great products to offer the consumer. But which ones are good, bad, ugly, or just an outright disaster?

Enter the salesperson: When you visit your local flooring store looking to purchase the right product for your job, you will be expecting the sales associate to sell you the most expensive be-all-and-ends-all laminate floor available. And in most cases, you will probably be right. We are trained to lead the customer from the most expensive to the least, depending on your budget. But in our defense, the most expensive laminate floors really are top quality with some of the best warranties available. So we really are selling you something that will last.

Enter the installer: To be honest, from the top-level laminate floors to the lowest end in price, the laminate flooring installation is basically the same in principle. They all have the click-lock tongue and groove interlocking system that connects each of the planks together. You can use the same installation tools. The layout would be the same. And you will probably spend the same amount of time installing them. However, you want to be on high-alert when considering the cheapest special-buy laminate floors, because the price may be great, but the entire installation could be a big nightmare!

A few years ago I got a call to install a laminate flooring for a friend. They had already got an "awesome deal" on the floor, and it laid in wait for me to get started "as soon as I could?" I would always get these kinds of calls from people I knew. And usually they are the jobs when I'm in and out in no time, and on to the next job.

I always start a job by clicking together a few of the planks as a practice right out of the box. This gives me a good idea on the quality of the flooring before I even start an install. Doing this also means that I only open one of the boxes and not the entire job, which would make it a nightmare to repackage and return if the flooring had an issue!

It was when I started to click a couple of the planks together from that first box that I noticed the finish was peeling off. Thinking that it could have been a problem with that box, I then tried it on another with a similar result. To be absolutely sure I was dealing with a monster of a laminate floor, I took my rubber hammer to it, only to see yet again the finish peeling off like sunburn! Safe to say that this was not the job I wanted to deal with. As a professional, I valued my work and took pride in each and every job I did. And this was just not going to work for me.

Enter the contractor / house flipper: I get it, you want to be in and out as fast as possible, and spend as little money as you can. Besides, you are just flipping the house and are sure the new owners will just replace it anyway. So how would you install a nightmare special-buy laminate floor?

Buy an extra 20 to 30% of flooring for waste, and just take your time when clicking the flooring together. You want to treat that flooring like a new-born baby. Also, wrap your rubber hammer, pull bar, and tapping block in duct tape or painters tape where it comes into contact with the floor. Doing this will absorb the direct blows to the floor, and will greatly decrease the amount of finish that will get damaged. Check out the picture in the "Tools For The Job" section to see an example of this method in-action.

Not every special-buy flooring is bad! And this is why it's always a good idea to either take a sample home, or buy one full box that you can test out when you get out of the store. In most cases the store will allow you to return it for a full refund.

Sections covered in this chapter are:
- Brands
- Style
- Finish - Thickness
- Finish - Laminate Layers
- In-Stock or Special Order
- Laminate Acclamation Time
- Laminate Samples
- Underlayment

Product Selection - Brands

Without doubt the most famous brand of laminate flooring is, Pergo. In fact, most customers think laminate flooring is called Pergo, and they just don't realize that this is just a brand name in that market. It's actually pretty hard to convince customers that other brands are available. But other brands do exist, and also produce a top quality product that is as good, if not better than Pergo. Here are some of the brands to start researching.

- Du-Pont Flooring
- Armstrong Flooring
- Bruce Flooring
- Hampton Bay Flooring
- Home Legend Flooring
- Allen Roth Flooring
- Mohawk Flooring
- Traffic Master Flooring

Another good tip is to ask friends or check laminate flooring forums for ideas on what the current top brands are. A lot of the time you can find reviews online at Amazon or Home Depot, which will give you an even better idea on quality and performance. But I always recommend people research online first before you hit the stores.

You can also buy laminate flooring online at many different outlets and websites. But most of the time people shy away from this because they just can't see the product up-close. However, some websites will actually send you a few free samples to your home so you can get a detailed look at that specific flooring. And this is a great way to get a hands-on look at the selections. But if you don't find free samples, then just be aware that the color on your computer monitor could be way off from what the color of the flooring will actually look like. But online shopping is a great way to find the deals that local stores do not offer. Just consider the shipping charges.

Also consider how long the brand has been around. Popular and established brands like Pergo have been around for years, and will be for many more to come. So you can be pretty safe in assuming any warranties will be honored, and that if you need to ever purchase more of the flooring in a few months down the road, the bigger companies will probably still stock it, or at least know where you can get it from.

Smaller and newer companies trying to make a name in the laminate flooring market may offer huge lifetime warranties, but who's to say they will be around in 65 years, 30 years, or even 5? And it's the smaller companies that usually turn over styles and designs much quicker than anyone else. Because they only survive on their next popular products sales. But please don't think I'm going after the "small guys", because you really can find some awesome deals with the smaller brands. And most of the time they are much more appreciative of your business. But just keep this in the back of your mind when you are researching what brand to buy from.

Product Selection - Style

Many different styles and colors are on offer in todays ever-growing laminate flooring market. Gone are the days of just one or two oak looking laminate floors that were just light, or dark. Now currently in 2013, you have more choices than ever before, which can sometimes make you feel overwhelmed at the thought of what one to buy. So let me break it down to make it as easy and less intimidating as possible for you.

As a sales associate I'm always helping people with the same dilemma you may currently find yourself in? Which style do you want? Obviously budget plays a big role in this decision, so that's always my first question to the customer to narrow down the selection a bit more. Now the next questions would be to find out it they are looking for a laminate that looks like wood, or tile? If you have not been out shopping the laminate flooring aisle yet, they now offer laminate flooring that looks just like ceramic, porcelain, travertine, and even marble tile. Shocking! ;-)

Let's take a look at both the wooden looking laminate flooring, and then tile options below.

Laminate Floors
by William Warby

Wooden Looking Laminate Flooring:

It may not be real wood of course, but the wooden looking laminate flooring is the next best thing to a real hardwood floor. They look just the same, some of them sound the same when you walk on them, and now most manufacturers even emboss the grain of wood right into the finish of the floor. They even feel the same when you run your hands over them. I've installed laminate flooring for people that I'm convinced still think that it's a real hardwood floor.

Most of the time the customer will select a nice looking, fair priced, natural wood style laminate floor.

And I don't blame them, because some of those floors look amazing. But let's not forget about the tile looking laminate flooring.

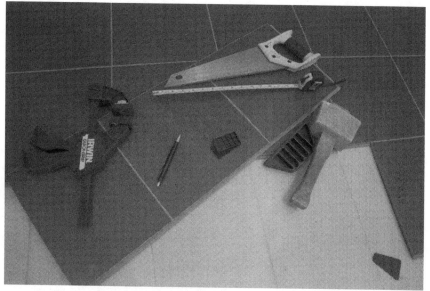

Tile Laminate Flooring
by cobaltfish

Tile Laminate Flooring:

Some wise laminate boffins somewhere decided to create a laminate flooring that looks just like a real tile floor! Who in the world would want to install that on their floors? A LOT OF PEOPLE!

Tile laminate floors were a big joke when they first came out into the laminate flooring market. Let's just say they left a little to the imagination to fully pull-off that authentic tile look. They began very plain-looking, no great detail, and super expensive. Now, things have changed in a big way and tile laminate has become a huge seller, and is starting to catch up to the sales of its wooden rival. This is because the manufacturers have simply done an amazing job recreating the look of real tile on a laminated board.

So many different styles and colors of tile laminate can be found in the aisles of your local flooring stores. They are attractive, warm to walk on(unlike real tile in the winter), and they even have embossed grout lines that perfectly resemble a real tile floor.

If you are looking for a real tile floor, but have issues with the high maintenance installation, and do not fancy frozen feet when you walk over it. Then laminate tile planks is probably going to blow you away when you finally get to see it. It's only when you see it first-hand that you really appreciate the detail of this kind of product.

The only caveat of picking a tile laminate flooring, is that with some styles you may have to take extra time on the installation matching up grout lines between planks, and then maybe playing around with pattern repeats on some of the more intricate stone looking laminates. But this is no where near as time-consuming as a real tile floor install. So do not fuss a little extra time being taken to install these amazing looking floors.

Style Conclusion:

You know what I always say to people? If you love the look of a particular laminate flooring style, and if it fits within your budget, please don't fret over a 15 year, 20 year, or lifetime warranty. Because if you think about it, who really keeps the same floor for 15 or 20 years in today's world? So don't lose sleep over one or the other just because of a warranty. They will both perform the same regardless of if they look like wood, or tile. Remember that the style of the flooring is just a picture under a protective coating, so it really makes no sense to think of durability as a decider between the two different styles. Just think about what you want, what would look good in your home, and what will make you happy to see every-time you enter that room.

Product Selection - Finish Thickness

Finish Thickness - (Ranges – 5mm to 15+mm):
The thickness of the plank in most laminate flooring is

measured in Millimeters(MM). This measurement is taken from the bottom of the entire plank to the very top. But the thickness is not always a sign of its durability, because that more depends on the protective wear coating that is applied to the top of the laminate during production. But thickness still plays an important role in the final quality of the laminate flooring.

Some people may tell you that the thickness of a laminate flooring will make a difference when heavy objects are dropped on them. But even if this may have a slight truth to it, it is not 100% correct. You may purchase a thick 12mm plank and think it is going to be indestructible. But if the core of the plank has been constructed from cheap materials, then that plank will crush just as easily as a 8mm or 10mm thickness.

Here are a few things that thicker planks can be good for:
- Better sound reduction.
- Some handle impact better.
- Cover very minor subfloor issues.
- Flex less, so overall wear is better.
- Sometimes a little easier to install.

More Tips On Laminate Thickness:
Keep in mind that some laminate flooring styles come

with an attached underlayment to the bottom of the plank, which is also included in the overall thickness measurement. You may think you're getting a 12mm thick plank, but it's only really 10mm thick with a 2mm thick underlayment(10mm(plank) + 2mm(padding) =12mm total). Something to keep in mind when you consider the thickness.

The thicker the floor usually means the more natural it will sound when walking on it, almost like you are walking on a real hardwood flooring. Thinner floors are usually more noisy because they tend to have more flexibility in them, which you may hear especially well in floors that have been installed over a less than level subfloor. But with this added thickness could come issues with floor height under cabinets, doorways, and of course you could be dealing with having to use different transition strips if meeting other floors at different heights.

Thickness Conclusion:
The thickness may be important to you, but the wear layer and build quality of that thickness should take precedence over everything else. If you want a durable floor you just can't go on the thickness measurement alone. But if you get a thick laminate floor with a good wear layer, solid core, and a nice warranty to back it all up, then that will not hurt at all.

Product Selection - Laminate Layers Explained

I like the analogy that you should think of a laminate flooring as a layered sponge cake, with the finish on top being the frosting. But this is not entirely correct, because usually on a cake the frosting holds all the color and decoration. But on a laminate flooring product, the finish is just a clear coat of protection that covers the layer that holds all the colors and detail.

Layers Of Laminate Explained:

Most laminate floors are constructed of four layers that when formed together produce one entire plank. It's the quality of each of these layers that can determine if your laminate flooring is going to be a winner, or a complete waste of time, and money.

Let's cover each layer separately.

Bottom Layer #1 - Melamine Plastic:

The bottom layer is a thin melamine plastic that adds

some durability to the bottom of the plank, as well as protect it against moisture from the subfloor. This is the layer you will never see, but that does not mean it is not an important part of the plank. This layer keeps anything under it away from the all-important core layer, so mild moisture, small debris, and anything else that you don't really want coming into contact with the core of the plank would be protected by this bottom layer.

Second Layer Up #2 - HDF Core:
The next layer up is the core of the plank which is usually constructed of a high-density fiberboard(HDF), that adds even more durability and moisture resistance to the middle of the laminate flooring. This is the meat of each plank and if quality materials are used, it can make all the difference in the world to the final product.

Third Layer Up #3 - Decorative Layer / Image Layer:
One more layer up we have the image or decorative layer, which is basically a hi-resolution photo of either wood or tile, and it sits above the core layer. The decorative layer includes all the colors and style designs that may be included in that particular laminate flooring.

The good thing about this layer is actually one of the main benefits of buying a laminate floor. Because it's basically a computer generated print that will not vary or change color between production runs, unlike its real wood counterpart. "So what?", I hear you say? Well, if you installed real wood flooring and didn't get added extras just incase, then six months down the line and you need to make a repair to a damaged section, when you go back to the store to purchase another box you may find a big difference in the shade/color of the finish. But with a computer generated laminate design you can be pretty sure it will match the flooring you previously purchased six months ago, almost exactly.

Forth Layer Up #4 - Top Of Plank - Wear Layer:
The finish or wear layer(top layer), is a very important part of the selection process when considering purchasing your laminate floor. Because it's this wear layer that will take all the direct hits, so to speak. Most wear layers contain an aluminum oxide protective coating that is applied over the decorative layer to keep it protected. Many of the laminate manufacturers have now created their own finish formulas that they apply to the flooring, and then they usually give it a cool sounding name like, per-guard or protect-tech finish. But it's pretty much the same thing to be honest.

As the final layer on a plank, it is this wear layer that

will make a big difference on the longevity of your floor. If it's constructed right, then you can be pretty safe in assuming that your flooring will stand up to some of the toughest use you can give it, within reason of course.

Pressing The Layers Together:

With all the layers ready to go, the manufacturer will then press them all together with huge hydraulic rams, and then basically bake them at high temperatures until done. It's at this point that they would add any textures or embossings to the laminate using special plates in order to get that magical detail into the flooring. The last step is to test the result by sticking a toothpick into the middle to check if it's done! Ok, a joke! But the manufacturing process can be a bit of a bore for some!;)

The Final Result:

The final quality of the laminate flooring will usually be reflected in how long of a warranty the manufacturer gives that flooring. So you can assume that a 5 year warranty on a laminate will not have a very thick wear protection on it, or have a very substantial core. But a product with a 25 year or even a lifetime warranty will have a pretty substantial protection on it, with extremely durable layers all the way through.

Below is a picture I put together of the different layers separated for easy viewing.

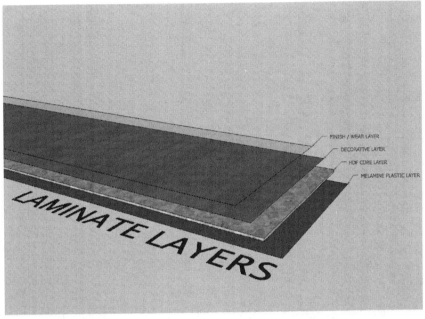

FINISH / WEAR LAYER
DECORATIVE LAYER
HDF CORE LAYER
MELAMINE PLASTIC LAYER

LAMINATE LAYERS

The different layers of laminate flooring.

Gloss / Matte Finish?

My last topic to cover in this section covers a common question I get from customers I'm installing for, and customers I'm selling to. What is better? Gloss? Or a Matte finish? This part of the product selection can sometimes confuse people because they usually see both finishes with the exact same warranty, and usually at the exact same price. For some reason many people think a gloss finish would be more durable than a matte looking floor. And this is probably because with a gloss style they can actually see the finish. But let me tell you that floors without the gloss still do have that same protection on it, which is just as durable as the gloss. So it basically comes down to what style you like, with just a couple of things to consider.

- **Gloss** - Looks newer - Shows dents/scratches easier - Easier to clean, but higher maintenance.
- **Matte** - Hides more imperfections - Less reflective - Dull finish.

Also remember that color makes a big difference as well.

Now you are educated in what the laminate layers are, and how they are made. You can now go to your local store and check them out for yourself.

In Stock Or Special Order?

If time is a factor when deciding what laminate flooring to buy, then you may want to select an in-stock product instead of something you have to special order. A downside of in-stock laminate flooring is the fact that you are usually only limited to the styles and colors the store decides to showcase in their showroom.

Special order laminate flooring can open a whole new world of color and style choices, sometimes too many to count. But if you have the time to wait, and in most cases do not mind paying a little more, then this might be the way to go for you?

Important tip:
Most stores will add a restocking fee of 15% or more if you have to return a floor you special ordered. You won't have to deal with this if it was an in-stock product because they can usually resell the returned flooring. But with special order laminate, if you don't want to get charged that 15% re-stocking fee, then it's critical you get an accurate measurement of your room so you are not left with extra cases of flooring that you will lose money on. Checkout the Room Layout section in this guide to make sure you get the right amount of flooring.

Laminate Acclamation

While you browse the laminate flooring brands and styles you may need to keep something in mind. Some laminate flooring will require an acclamation period before you attempt to install it. What this means is that you have to place the boxes of flooring in the room you are going to install it, or in another room at a similar temperature for up to 48 to 72 hours. Now, this depends on what laminate you buy, and in some cases your flooring may not even need an acclamation time. But if it does, then this time allows the flooring to get acclimated to the temperature of the room, which can avoid excessive expansion and contraction that may cause issues with your flooring when it's completed.

Make sure you read the directions in the boxes of the flooring, and take into account the extra time needed if you are on a tight time frame. However, as I said above, some brands of laminate do not need this acclamation time at all, which means you can take it home and get to work right away.

Product Selection - Laminate Flooring Samples

The last thing I want to cover in the product selection is about samples. As an installer I don't really deal with samples because the customer has usually done this part of the process for themselves. But as a sales rep, I get to see this part of the process all the time.

So here are some tips about laminate flooring samples, and why they could be extremely useful!

The first thing about laminate flooring samples is that they are usually free to take, depending on where you go to look at the flooring. And although sometimes small, you can still get a good look at the color of the floor sample in your home. "Why is that important?", because it's all about the lights. In the local store you will probably be under some kind of a fluorescent lighting, which can make the flooring appear a slightly different color/shade from the light at your home.

I've had many customers actually bring back laminate flooring boxes, because when they got it home it just didn't match the wall colors, or cabinet colors, or trim colors and so on. This is one of the biggest reasons paint stores offer small light boxes to place paint samples in, just so you can test them in different light configuration before you paint a wall. Yes, it may mean an extra trip back and forth to the store, but you will be doing that anyway if you have to return the flooring.

The second thing about laminate samples is the fact that you can take them home and really test out that durability! Try and see how good that finish really is. Scratch it, try to dent it, chip it, peel at it, and in general put it through its paces. Remember that you should only be looking to do things to it that would normally happen in a real home, so don't go crazy and rent a jack-hammer or drive over it. But who knows, maybe it will survive? This is a great testing opportunity before you go ahead and buy a laminate floor. And of course, if you just put down a $25 deposit on a sample, please don't try this step unless you want the store to keep your money. But no harm in asking them for a scrap piece.

Samples are important! So take as many as you can get!

Product Selection - Underlayment

Laminate flooring, unlike real hardwood flooring, requires an underlayment padding to absorb and cushion the foot traffic over the top of it. Because of the floating nature of laminate, and the fact that it is usually independent and not attached to the subfloor, it tends to move about much more than something that is attached to the subfloor with nails or glue. So an underlayment is used to protect this movement and flexing from stressing the tongue and groove joints between all the planks.

A visit to the local flooring store will probably involve you walking down the aisle to a few different types of laminate flooring underlayment, which can range from really cheap, to pretty expensive. It can all be pretty overwhelming trying to gauge what one would be the best-bet for your own project. So let me break it down for you.

Laminate Underlayment Selection

Basic Level Underlayment: Price Range - $

A basic cheap level underlayment would be a very thin layer of foam and that's about it. This does its job for contractors or home owners that are looking to not invest a lot of money, because maybe they are selling the place after? Or they may only be looking for a temporary solution for a flooring that they will change in a few months down the road.

You have to be careful when purchasing a very basic bottom-of-the-line underlayment, because some laminate flooring manufacturers will void a warranty if the underlayment underneath their flooring is under the basic recommendations. But if you are flipping the house and do not care about the warranty, then by all means consider it as an option. But keep in mind the poor new owners!

One thing to note here for those of you flipping or selling a house, and are thinking of doing in on-the-cheap, think about this. In most cases the flooring manufacturers will actually honor a warranty even if it is passed on to the new owners. This can be a huge selling point for you, because you can basically tell the new owners that the flooring is brand-spanking new, and is also covered by a large warranty that they now own. But you have to use the recommended products to install the flooring in the first place. Sure, it might cost you a little more at first, but if it results in pleasing a possible new owner then it may well be money well spent.

2 in 1 Underlayment: Price Range - $$

When you see a 2 in 1 underlayment, what you are basically buying is an underlayment that has two different layers of protection rolled into one roll. One of the layers will be a moisture/vapor barrier that protects the underside of the laminate flooring from rising moisture. And the other layer will be a standard foam cushioning to protect the laminate seams during daily use.

The 2 in 1 underlayment is probably the most popular because of its price, which usually runs about $20-$30 for a 100sf roll. It's also one of the paddings that the flooring manufacturers are ok with, meaning that you get to keep that all important warranty.

This kind of underlayment will usually be about 2mm thick, and will be fine for installations on-grade or below-grade(basements). But one thing to remember here if you plan on purchasing this underlayment in a basement with a concrete/cement subfloor, is that you must still use a poly film vapor barrier underneath it. Even though this underlayment comes with one already, manufacturers still want you to add the extra poly film below their products.

3 in 1 Underlayment: Price Range - $$$

This kind of underlayment as you may have guessed has three different layers rolled into one. And within this 3 in 1 product can be a couple of variations of the layers that are used. Below is a quick overview of the layers you may find in your local stores.

- Vapor Barrier / Foam / Reflective Film: 3 in 1:
This 3 in 1 underlayment comes with a reflective film layer that enhances its radiant thermal properties. So it in theory should help with heat escape, and may keep the cold out a little better than the standard underlayment.

With a pretty impressive price range from, $40 to $55 for a 100 square foot roll, this is slightly more of an investment than most of the others. But you may get that cost reflected back in your heating bills?

- Vapor Barrier / Polyshims / Plastic Sheets
An underlayment built for air-flow. This type of product is usually best where moisture could be a concern for you. The polyshim design allows air flow underneath the underlayment, and at the same time utilizes micro-ban antimicrobial technology that inhibits mold and mildew growth.

Some of the air-flow underlayment also come with sound suppression characteristics, which cut down on the foot traffic noise. So this type of roll would be a pretty good all-round choice.

Sound Blocking Underlayment:
Some sound-blocking underlayment may be included in a 2 in 1 or 3 in 1 product above. But you may also find that you come across one specifically for sound reduction. The deal with sound-reducing underlayment

is to not only dampen the sound between floors, but to also make your laminate flooring sound like the real wood flooring when people walk on it. One big criticism I get with laminate flooring is that it sounds plastic when people walk on it. Well, this type of product is your answer.

If you are looking for a laminate flooring to not only look like real wood, but to also sound like it? Then this product would be your best choice.

Underlayment Wrap-up:
New underlayment arrives on the market every single week recently it seems. From moisture controlled, to sound reducing, to felt mufflers, and even air flowing kinds! It can at times be harder to pick an underlayment than it can the flooring! But take a breath and figure out what you want from your underlayment. And always remember what the flooring manufacturer recommends as a minimum.

Most flooring stores will have displays that you can actually touch or test out. This type of display can be very handy to give you a great idea on how each of the underlayment's perform. And of course you can always ask someone that works in that store, or shoot me an email if you have any questions(email at the end of guide)!

Underlayment Attached,

Or Not?

Some laminate flooring brands feature an attached underlayment on the bottom side of the plank. While others expect you to grab the padding separately at the same time you buy the floor, and then give you requirements on what underlayment to purchase with it.

So what's the pro's and cons of attached or un-attached underlayment?

First with the underlayment attached:

Underlayment already attached to flooring.

For obvious reasons this approach means you only need to buy the boxes of flooring, and not have to worry about choosing a separate manufacturer recommended underlayment to go under it. It's also a step saved while installing the laminate, because you do not have to put it down on the subfloor before you start to install it. So It's a time saver!

Another benefit of attached underlayment is that it is glued directly to the back of the planking, whereas separate planking and underlayment on a not so flat subfloor can cause a slight rise and separation between the two surfaces in areas, and although this is not going to ruin the floor, you may start to hear some noise when they move separately.

And finally, as the manufacturer chose the underlayment, you will always know it's the right one for the job and not just some cheap thin piece of junk!

Unattached underlayment:

No underlayment attached - Sold separately.

This adds another step to the installation process by making you lay some padding first before you start laying the planks. But it really is not that much of a burden to be honest, and takes very little time to do.

Unattached also means you get to choose your underlayment. Many stores now have more than one style to pick from, and you may not want to be limited to a generic padding chosen by the manufacturer. You may need a padding that has a noise reduction in it, or a vapor gap to allow air to circulate under the flooring. But at least with unattached underlayment, you have that option.

Side-note: Because of the multiple underlayment

choices on offer, you may still want to check with the manufacturer just to make sure that the one you purchase will still hold-up that warranty. Usually most laminate flooring cases will have a toll-free number on, so you can at least ask questions directly to the company that makes it.

What do I use? I usually just pick a laminate flooring that I like, and if it does not have the underlayment attached I'll just pick up a mid-range type, or one specifically for a location like in a basement, and that's always worked fine for me. But at the end of the day, now that you know all about the underlayment, your choice should be a little easier than it was before.

Tools For The Job

Get the right tools for the job? The beauty of laminate flooring is just how easy it is to install. And that also means you do not need a room full of tools to do it. But knowing the right tools for the job is a great way to start any installation.

Before we start breaking down the various tools to use when installing a laminate flooring, I want to list a few of the tools you will need, as well as optional products and safety equipment that will make your laminate flooring installation a much easier task.

Needed:
- Rubber Hammer.
- Regular Hammer.
- Pry Bar (Moulding).
- Mask - When cutting floor.
- Goggles - When Cutting floor.
- Saws.

Optional:
- Knee Pads.
- Gloves.
- Foot Covers.

○   Contour Gauge.

Sections covered in this chapter are:
- ○   Install Kits
- ○   Saws
- ○   Contractor Tooling Tips

Tools For The Job - Install Kits

The installation kits are pre-packaged boxes of the tools you will need to install the floor. And usually they will come with the following.

- ○   Tapping Block
- ○   Pull Bar
- ○   Spacers
- ○   *Moisture Tester

* Only in certain kits.

Let me cover each tool individually, so you will have an idea on how to use each one in the box.

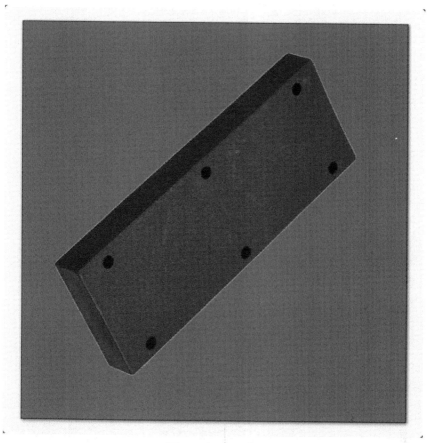

Tapping Block

Tapping Block: A tapping block would be needed to lightly tap together the longest edge of one plank into the other(pictured below), or on the ends if you have enough space. So if on the first attempt to click the planks together you are left with a tiny gap between boards, you just prop the tapping block gently on the plank, and then tap them together using a rubber mallet on the block until the gap closes.

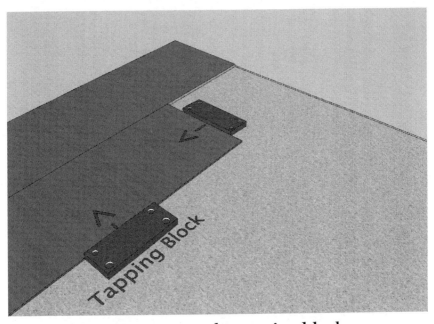

Ways to use the tapping block.

Tapping blocks are also handy for areas where a plank cannot be rotated into place. Areas like under a door-frame, or under heating elements that run along the room are common situations where a good tapping block can pay for itself.

Pull Bar

Pull-Bars: Pull-bars are usually used when you do not have enough space to either click the floor together, or use a tapping block. And this is common when you are restricted for space by walls, or if you have to reach under heating elements that you cannot access with a tapping block. But it's the same idea as a tapping block because you just hook one side of the pull-bar on the end of a plank(Pictured below), then lightly tap the partially open gaps together.

Pull-bar in action.

As you can see from the image above. A pull-bar is perfect for the areas that cannot be reached by the tapping block.

Spacers

Spacers: Pre-measured plastic spacers are usually included in the install kit so that you have something to keep the expansion gap around the perimeter. They are usually pre-set at 1/4" on one end, and 3/8" on the other. So depending on what the manufacturer recommends for an expansion gap on your floor, you just have to flip the spacer either way and place around the perimeter to keep that particular spacing.

Moisture Tester: Some of the install kits on offer

will also come with a moisture tester. It might be as simple as a 2'x2' poly sheet, but it will help you get a good idea on how much moisture you may be dealing with before you install the laminate flooring. Newer install kits are now actually coming with moisture testers with gauges on them, so you know exactly what readings you are dealing with. But I've not really seen a great deal of them around, and they are usually a few dollars more than the basic install kits. But worth it to put your mind at rest if moisture is a concern for you.

For around $20 for an install kit, it really is a good purchase to make before installing a laminate floor. Most of the kits come with all the basic tools you need when installing a laminate flooring. And most of the manufacturers recommend using them in the process of doing so. But a bit later in this section, I do recommend a few tips and cheats to use for those of you that do not want to invest in a good install kit.

Tools For The Job - Saw Selection

In order to cut the laminate flooring you have a few

options available to you. In this section I wanted to cover a few different saw options to get the job done without any issues.

Here are a few options.

Table Saw / Mitre Saw:

A good table saw or mitre saw will make cutting the laminate flooring a breeze. But in order to get a nice clean cut you need to have the right blade. Most hardware stores offer what they call a laminate blade that is specifically for laminates. But if you can't find one, then a good carbide-fibre tip blade with a higher tooth count(80-100) will work just fine. But always ask someone at the store if you are not too sure. And depending on the size of your job, or how many rooms you are doing, you may still need extra blades because laminate flooring can be really tough on them.

Jigsaw:

A jigsaw is often used when cutting notches out of the laminate flooring. This is a perfect tool to use when you need to cut around pipes, heaters, wires, and other items that just need a small piece taken out of a plank. Again, you can get specific laminate blades for your jigsaw at the local store. One thing to keep in mind is that cutting with a jigsaw is pretty much always freehand, so a steady-hand is always a good thing when using one.

Circular Saw with rip guide:

I've seen some installers use only a circular saw to cut everything they need to get the job finished. They cut the planks with it, notch out around pipes with it, and even use it for the moulding, it really is a sight to see! But for the average homeowner this is probably a little extravagant, and if you can get hold of the right tools listed above, it will make your life a little easier. But a circular saw is always a good option, and a rip-guide will make the cuts look a little more professional. A lot of this will also be free hand, so it's important to keep those cuts nice and straight.

Floor Boar & other dust free cutting tools:

A few dust-free laminate flooring cutting tools are floating around that you may have seen at the local store. By dust free, I mean that these tools rely on the power of you, and are not plugged into any wall outlets. You just simply line up the cut you need to make, and then pull a handle down that drops a blade almost like a guillotine into the flooring. This method is not used as much as the power saws, but I still wanted to cover it as an option for you. You will still need a jigsaw incase you come up with any areas where you need to take a notch out of a plank. But for people not wanting to deal with all the sawdust, the dust-free cutters are a great way to go.

Undercut saws / Jamb Saw:

One of the most time-consuming parts of installing laminate flooring can be cutting under the moulding and door frames, especially when you do not want to remove them or don't have any choice to do so. The use of an undercut saw will make this job a lot more easier for you, especially if it's electric. If you use the manual power undercut saws then obviously it will take a while longer. But at least it's better than using something else that is just not fit for the job.

Tools For The Job - Contractor Tooling Tips

Most flooring installers already have all the bells and whistles needed to install the floor. But some of them have shared with me some great little tooling tips over the years, that I've personally put into practice. I'll share with you a few of these tips so you have a head start over most DIY'ers.

Padded Tape:

One tip I love to use is to take either duct tape, painters tape, or padded tape, and apply it to the end of my rubber mallet, hammer, pull bar, and tapping block. As I said in an earlier chapter, this can cushion a direct blow to the finish on the laminate flooring and cut down on any chips or dents. This is especially helpful when dealing with lower end laminates with a much thinner finish.

My own taped tools ready for action.

Waste Spacers:

It can be a little annoying to keep track of all the

small black spacers you need to keep the expansion gap around the perimeter of the flooring. They usually come pre-packaged in the install kit, but as soon as you use them for one job, a few vanish. Then you are left with only a small collection of them which can be a real pain to use. So, a good trick is to use some small waste pieces of the floor you are installing as the spacers. Simply wedge the cut pieces of laminate flooring around the perimeter as you go, and you never have to buy another box of spacers. Just make sure the gap is the recommended size.

Another point regarding spacers is to use painters tape to tape the spacers to the wall so they don't move around(pictured below). Get a delicate painters tape just so it doesn't peel any paint or wallpaper off the wall after you are done with them.

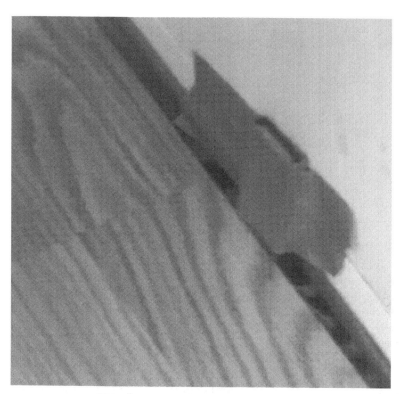

Wedge spacers taped to wall.

Room Layout

One part of a flooring installation that confuses people the most is the room layout, area size, and how much flooring to buy. I want to make this section as easy as possible so that you will spend less time worrying about how much flooring to get, and more time on the install part of it.

Looking at the layout of a room can stop people from trying to do it themselves. Either it looks too intimidating, or more like a lot of hard work. Either way you look at it, if you know what to do you can break it down into sections, and then tackle a little at a time. It does not have to be rocket-science.

Sections covered in this chapter are:
- Planning Your Layout.
- How Many Square Feet.

Room Layout - Planning Your Layout

When working with customers in the store, one of the most common questions I get is, "I'm not too sure how much flooring to get?" They would then present a hand-drawn box on a piece of paper that I think represented their room? Occasionally, you would get some dimensions on this paper either in inches, feet, and sometimes even in metric sizes. But I always felt that it was a great thing to see them wanting to try an install themselves. And I always hoped that if given a choice they would take up flooring installation as a hobby, and not drawing! ;)

It actually is a good idea to draw a basic shape of the room you want to install your flooring in. Or if you are pretty good with a computer, you can use that to draw an outline of your rooms. This gives you a birds-eye view of the area as well as any issues you may come up against, even in a basic drawing.

The first step we shall take is to draw a basic layout of the room from a birds-eye view. For this example I'll use a pretty common and simple layout, but one that can cause a lot of problems if the measurements are not correct. I usually use a simple computer program to outline my rooms, as in the example we will use below.

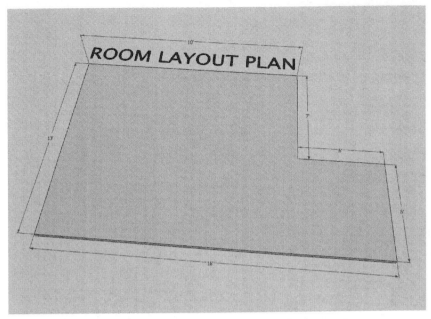

Full room view - One entire section

As you can see from the image above, we basically have a rectangular room with a box cut out of one corner. Don't worry about the measurements in the image just yet, as this is just an example to showcase how to easily break down a room into smaller sections.

Box Method:

What you will notice in the layout of our example room, is a basic shape with some measurements around each wall. This can get really confusing for first-time installers, because it just seems like a lot of work to figure out the room size. But if you use this box method, it actually makes it pretty easy to break down.

What we will do next is break this room down into two different sections using boxes. This will make it even easier to measure the area size. In the image below I divided the room up into two squares(boxes), one big(1), and one small(2). And even though it is in the same room without any dividers, I always tell people to use this method to make it a lot easier to get an accurate room size.

If you have a basic square room then you are pretty much set to move on to the next section at this point. But you may want to follow along, just in case you ever come up against a room similar to the one in our example.

Divided up into two sections

With our room now broken down into two boxes, we only have to measure the two sections separately to get the total square feet of each separate box, then just add them together to get the total square feet for that entire area.

If you have a room with different shapes like the image below, you can still section the different areas up into squares or rectangle shapes, which will make it easier to measure for you. Even if you have curves in the room you can still use this technique, just like I have done in the example below.

Divided up into three section because of an added curve.

As you can see from the image, my room now has a couple of new curves added to it. But I can still use the box method even on this curved layout by simply adding another box around section 3. And as section 2 has an indented-curve, I can leave box(2) just as it is. This just means I'm a little over on the area size sometimes. But I'd rather be over than under and not have enough laminate to finish my floor, and it's never a huge amount extra anyway.

Box Method Breakdown:

The box method is a really valuable and easy technique to break down odd-shaped rooms into bite-sized sections. Just because you may not have any walls separating certain areas, does not mean you can't divide a room up to make it easier on yourself. This method makes a task that you may find the most daunting, to actually become a pretty simple undertaking if you approach it the right way.

Now we have the room all boxed up! In the next section we will start to deal with the actual room measurements. And then finally get your rooms square foot totals.

Room Layout - How Many Square Feet?

Taking our divided room layout from the previous section, we will now start to work out each sections size. It is actually pretty easy to work out how many square feet you have in a room. But if you listen to some people, they can really confuse you with all the different ways to do it.

How To Measure An Areas Size:

All you need to do is grab a tape measure, and then measure(up) from one side of the room to the other(down) in a straight line. Then write that measurement down on your room plan in the same location on the paper. Now repeat the same step from the other side(left) of the room to its opposite wall(right). To work out the square feet, just multiply the two measurements together and you have your square foot area size.

As an example, let's start with box #1 from our previous layout.

ROOM LAYOUT PLAN

13x10= 130sf

1

13'

10'

Section 1 is 13 feet by 10 feet.

Box #1: Was 13 feet down one wall by 10 feet down the other wall. So to get our square foot area for section 1, all I did was multiply 13x10.

13'x10' = 130sf (square feet) for section #1.

Box #2: I just repeated the same method as I did for the first area of the room. Measure from one side to the other from each end of the room, and then write down the measurements.

Section 2 is 6 feet by 6 feet.

Section 2 was a basic box of 6 feet by 6 feet. We can ignore that inner curve in the room. Because by boxing it off and including it in section 2, will compensate for that area.

6'x6' = 36sf (square feet) for section #2.

Box #3: Last but not least is section #3, which is that outer curved area that joins section #2. But as we boxed this area off in the previous section, all we have to do is measure in a rectangle around it.

Section 3 is 6 feet by 3 feet - After I boxed it in.

Section 3 is that outer curved area. So to box it off I just measure from the longest length of the curve which is the back in this example. I came up with 6 feet. Then I measured from the most outer part of the curve back, to get 3 feet.

6'x3' = 18sf (square feet) for section #3.

With all of the three sections(boxes) now completed. And with each of the areas total square feet measurements in hand. It's time to add them all together to get the entire areas square feet measurement.

- o Section1 = 130sf
- o Section2 = 36sf
- o Section3 = 18sf

130 + 36 + 18

=

Total Square Feet: 184

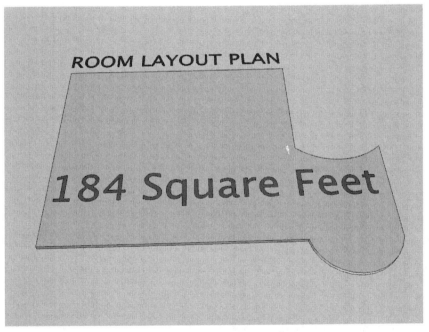

184 Total square feet.

Adding Extra Material For Waste:

When buying your laminate flooring it's always a good idea to buy at least an extra 5 to 10% more for waste, cuts, mistakes, and anything else unplanned that may occur. So when taking my 184sf room total, all I need to do is add 10% to it, making a new grand total of

202sf. Let's just round it down to 200 square feet.

184 + 10% = 202.4 (200 square feet rounded-down)

Ok, now if you followed this method along with your own room, you should now know exactly how much laminate you need to buy at the store. Just let the sales people know that you already added 10% for waste, just so they don't add anything extra to your totals.

Cool Design Ideas

Even if you are on a budget, you can still do some pretty cool looking things with laminate flooring! Most of the time customers come up to me and just want to purchase their flooring and be done with it. However, some are looking for a way to jazz that plain old laminate flooring up a bit, and give it that "wow" look when people visit. If this is you? Then check out this section on some cool design ideas that you can do yourself. And if done right, it does not have to cost you a lot more than you are already paying.

It's super-simple to do!

Sections covered in this chapter are:
○ Plank Stripes

Cool Design Ideas - Plank Stripes

Stripe Those Planks!
Ok, so here is a little trick to make your flooring look like a million dollars, and it hardly costs you any extra money to do it!

When you settle on which brand, style, and color of flooring you want in your room. You might want to consider purchasing a couple of cases of a contrasting color of the same style to use as stripes on your floor. Take a look at the picture below to see what I mean.

One Stripe

As you can see this is such a simple and cool looking thing to do! And you can use more than one stripe to make that flooring really pop.

Two Stripes Either Side

Two Stripes A Row Apart

Three Stripes Together On One Side

I can't tell you how many customers love the look of this technique, but had no idea it could be done, and how little it costs to do it. But you do have to keep some things in mind if this is what you want to do in your own rooms.

Same Brand/Style:

You must make sure the two colors are from the same brand and style as each other. And the reason is that different brands will have different tongue and groove systems, so they will usually not fit from one brand to the other. Sometimes even different styles of the same brand can differ. So make sure you ask the sales associate, or take a couple of the samples and click them together to make sure it's the perfect fit. Also, call the manufacturer to make double-sure this is an option, especially if you are going to special order the flooring.

The Installation

Now we hit the ground running and are ready to start the install. You should now have your laminate flooring picked out, acclimated, and ready to roll. I will now cover the entire install process in three easy to follow steps, that any first-time laminate flooring installers can follow along with.

- Step #1 - Prepping The Floor
- Step #2 - The Installation
- Step #3 - Moulding & Transitions

Other sections covered in this chapter are:
- Additional Layouts Explained
- Math Haters Unite

The Installation - Step #1 - Prep The Floor

"It's all in the prep!"

It's now time to get started with your install. By this time you should have your laminate ready and acclimated, the underlayment if not attached should be at-hand, and you should also have all the tools necessary to get this job done.

The first thing I do when starting an install is to prepare the room for the laminate flooring. This is one of the most important parts to do right, because it could save you a bunch of time further into the install, and make the entire process go a lot smoother.

Let's get this started! ;)

Remove Baseboard Molding / Existing Flooring:
If you have current flooring and moulding in the room it is now time to remove it. Usually the best way to start this is to remove the moulding from around the perimeter of the room first, because they are usually placed on top of the flooring after it is put down. It's wise to take them off now so that when you do pull the current flooring up, the moulding does not impede the process.

The best way to remove moulding is to use a pry-bar to get behind it, and then gently pull them away from the wall every few inches. As you start to go along in a line repeating this process, the moulding should become loose from the wall, and allow you to pull it completely away.

Make sure you do not dent the wall at this point because you do not want any unnecessary damage that you will have to fix later. So, if possible grab something soft and place it between the wall and your pry-bar. Doing so cuts down on a lot of the damage that you want to avoid.

Removing Carpet:

For those of you with carpet down, you will also have to remove the tack strips and any nails or staples that could tear the laminate underlayment, or even the back of the new laminate flooring. This can be a big pain, especially if you have hundreds of staples or nails sticking up. But it will save your flooring in the long run.

If you just cannot remove the nails or staples, then make sure you drive them into the subfloor with a hammer. As long as nothing is sticking up or raised when you are done, then you are in good standing for the next step.

Removing Tile / Sheet Vinyl / VCT Tile:

If you currently have ceramic tile, sheet vinyl, or VCT tile on your floor. Check with the manufacturers specifications because you might be able to install a laminate flooring over the top of it, without having to remove it first. If not, then you have to remove if from your subfloor before we progress.

With ceramic tile you could be looking at a time-sapping removal process ahead. Unfortunately removing ceramic tile, or any glued down tile like VCT can be a frustrating procedure, and generally means scraping up the tile and adhesive with a large floor scraper. Sometimes I find it best to break the tiles with a hammer first, then just scrape up the pieces all the way across the room.

Because of the thin-set mortar under a regular tile, the removal process could tear up the subfloor a bit! Which means that when this material is finally removed, you will need to patch up the damaged with a floor leveler to make sure it's flat enough again to handle a laminate flooring.

Sheet vinyl can either be glued down or floated like a laminate flooring. If you find that it is glued down, you might have a hard time removing it from the subfloor. But try to pull up as much as you can, because some hardware stores offer an adhesive removal product that makes it a lot easier to do. But the only thing is that you need to be able to get to the adhesive in order for it to work, so you still have to peel off the top layer. If the vinyl is floating, then it's as simple as pulling it back up and taking it out the room. But again the baseboard moulding should be removed first.

I find it easier to cut the sheet vinyl in sections from one side of a room to the other. This means that I only need to deal with a thinner strip, and not an entire sheet of vinyl.

Undercut Door Jamb Casing / Any Remaining Moldings:

With all the flooring removed and only the subfloor remaining, it's now time to start on the door casing and any other moulding you have left over.

Before you start on this step, you should take a small piece of your laminate flooring and add some underlayment underneath it. You will combine the two together because you will be taking this piece over to the doorways, and checking to see if it will slide under the door casings. If it does not slide under, or is too tight, you will need to use an undercut saw or jamb saw to remove some of the door casing. Just make sure you add 1/16" of space on top of the laminate and underlayment to make sure it does not bind, or impede the floor from moving after it's installed.

You may have an issue when you cannot remove the baseboard moulding, or have areas where some still remains. If this is the case you will need to follow the step above all the way around the room to cut a space under it. And remember that you still have to allow another 1/16" of clearance above the laminate and underlayment to allow it to move.

Using scrap laminate and padding as a guide to cut doorway

Make sure to add a little extra gap to allow it to slide under ok.

Adjust Door Height:

You may find that even a door has to be adjusted to allow the laminate underneath it. If this is true for you, it's best to remove the door and trim off the bottom of it. But this time make sure you remove an extra 1/8" of space above the laminate and underlayment to allow the door to open and close freely.

Vacuum, Dust & Remove Debris:

The last step of the prep is to remove any dust and debris from the subfloor. The best thing to do is vacuum up any remaining saw dust with a Shop Vac or something similar. But if all you have is a regular vacuum then that's perfectly fine. But just make sure in the final inspection that everything is completely clean and clear.

End Of The Prep:

With your flooring and moulding removed, and doors all trimmed and adjusted, we will now move on to the part you have been waiting for the most. The install! However, it never hurts to do another quick once-over of the subfloor to make double-sure everything looks as it should. With that said….. Let's move on!

The Installation - Step #2 - The Install

Now we are at the point when it's time to start putting your laminate flooring down. Everything is prepped and ready to go. So let us get right into the action and finally begin to put this flooring down!

In this section I'll be using a mixture of real pictures, as well as images I've put together on my own computer. I really wanted to show you the install in the most detail I could. So by using my computer generated images, I could really give you a much better, and clearer picture of the entire process.

This is basically how I undertake each laminate flooring installation I do. Every installer has other ideas and techniques that they use on a job, and that's great. But I want to share with you what I think is the most simple and easiest to follow technique that I can. At the end of the day I hope you pick up something extra of your own while you attempt this install, and I would really like you to share it with me! Use this section as a reference and a basic guideline, but feel free to adjust and adapt anything you wish along the way that will make your own installation even easier.

Good luck! ;)

Where To Start?
Lots of first-time installers ask me this question, "Where do we start the install?", and I can see the confusion. But a general rule-of-thumb is to lay the planks with the long side parallel to the longest wall(pictured below). If sunlight is a concern you can always lay the planks parallel to the incoming light source as well.

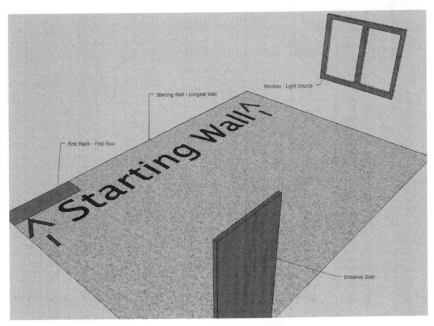

Starting Wall

The Expansion Gap:

One of the most important rules when installing a laminate flooring is the expansion gap. You must leave at least 3/8" of space around the perimeter of your laminate flooring to allow for expansion and contraction. If you do not leave this critical space you will be looking at all kinds of problems that can, and will, ruin your installation. This is why I wanted to put this in your mind right at the start!

MIND THE GAP!

Some laminate flooring brands may use a different gap size. But whatever it is, please obey it! And if all else fails and you just don't know what it could be? Play it safe and go with 3/8".

Install Step #1: The Moisture Barrier & Laying The Underlayment(if not attached already)

Concrete / Crawl Space Subfloor:

To begin the install for those of you with a concrete subfloor or installing over a crawl space, we need to first lay down the 6mil polyethylene sheet over the subfloor. This is actually a pretty simple step because all you have to do is roll the sheet of poly out over the entire floor. Make sure you allow a little extra to go slightly up the walls about an extra 2", because we will cut it better to size after the laminate flooring is down.

If the poly film you buy is not an entire sheet, but instead it comes in a long linear roll like the underlayment. Then you will have to put it down in overlapping rows. Once one row is down, and before the underlayment and flooring is completely covering the poly sheet, you should roll down the second row making sure you overlap the seams by about 8". Then all you have to do is use some duct tape to tape the two overlapping sheets of poly together, which will keep that seam from allowing any moisture to leak through it.

Time For The Underlayment:

Now we are ready to install the underlayment if it's not already pre-attached to your laminate flooring. To begin this step you just need to take the underlayment roll and lay it on the subfloor with the correct side facing up(the padding usually identifies what side is up and what side is down). Next just roll it over the subfloor in a single row from one side of the room to the other(pictured below).

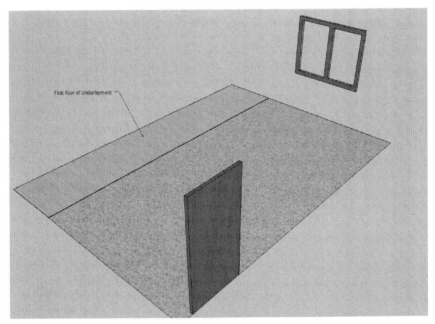

First row of underlayment put down.

Most of the current underlayment available now comes with an overlap strip that will have a peel and stick self-adhesive tape on it. If it does, then you want that edge of the underlayment to be facing the direction you will be moving across the room. This means that when you are ready to roll out the next row, you will then be able to stick the two rows together using this strip.

We only want to lay one row of underlayment at a time at this point, because if you do the entire room before you start putting down the planks, you will be walking all over it. and it will be sliding and moving all over the place under your feet. But for now, don't remove the self-adhesive strip until you are ready to put the next row down. Also make sure when you cut the underlayment you leave a little extra running up the walls at the ends, because we will cut it better to size after the entire floor is installed.

If your underlayment does not come with a self-adhesive overlap strip, then check the directions of the one you purchased. Some manufacturers recommend you overlap their products and fasten the seams with duct tape, and others recommend you butt them together and then apply some tape. So make sure you check before you continue.

Now you have your first row of underlayment down, it's time to start your first row of laminate flooring!

Working Out The Number Of Rows

<u>For those of you that hate measuring and math, goto "Math Haters Unite"</u>.

We are now ready to put down the first couple of rows of laminate flooring. But before we get to that we need to do a little math to work out the number of rows we will need. Most laminate flooring manufacturers recommend that you do not use a laminate plank that is less than a 2-1/2" wide strip. Which is no big deal, right? Not at the start of your install it's not, but what about the last row? If you get right to the other end of the room and then find out you need to cut a plank to less than 2-1/2" wide, you could be in trouble. So we will take care of that now. It's actually pretty simple to do!

Step 1) Grab a tape measure and measure from the wall you are starting at, to the opposite wall where you will be laying the final row of laminate. Make a note of the measurement(My example room is 13' feet across).

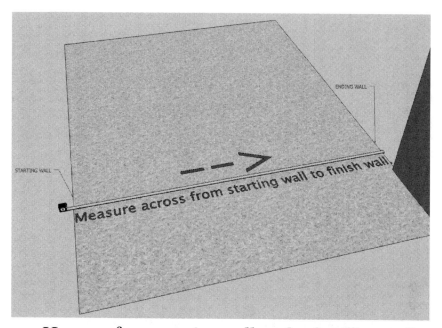

Measure from starting wall to the finishing wall. 13' feet across in this room.

Step 2) Now measure the width of one laminate flooring plank(My planks = 9").

Step 3) The next step is to divide the measurement of the room(step 1 = 13') by the measurement of the plank(step 2 = 9"). But first we need to convert those measurements into inches on our calculators.

For example, if my room was 13 feet across. I would multiply 13 x 12 to turn feet into inches(12 inches for every foot), and get **156"**. No matter what measurement you have from step 1, always multiply it by 12.

Now if my plank was only 9"? Because that measurement is under a foot I will not need to multiply it by 12 as I did with my room width measurement. So now all I would need to do is divide my room width by my plank width like this.

$$156" / 9" = 17.33$$

So I now know my room will be needing 17 full rows of planking, and .33(1/3) of a plank which is just under 3" on a 9" plank. The eagle-eyed among you will probably be yelling, "Ya, but what about the expansion gap!", and you would be right! If we have a 3" strip of planking and still need to deduct 3/8" twice(3/8" gap for each end), we would be at 3/4". So now our 3" plank would be 2 1/4" wide and under the 2 1/2" minimum for our particular flooring(check your own flooring directions to see if this measurement would be acceptable).

If your final row of planking is under the recommended minimum like in the example above, then please read the next section to correct this. If however you're safe and over the minimum, or only need to use full planks(lucky you), you can skip the next section and move on to "Let's Get Started."

Working Out The Numbers Of Row(s) - If Under Minimum Plank Width

We just found out from the previous section that we need to adjust our flooring in order to make sure we don't end up with a final row of planking under 2 1/2" wide. So we need to make an adjustment to our first row of planking to split the difference between the first and last row. What we will need to do here is trim down the first row of planking in order for us to make sure our final row is above the 2 1/2" minimum. Let's work out how to do that right now!

What we know:

○   We know that we need 17.33 rows of laminate flooring to get from one side of the room to the other.

○   We also know that the .33(1/3 of plank) + expansion gaps(3/8"x2 =3/4") would only leave us with a 2 1/4" final row.

○   We know that 2 1/4" is under our 2 1/2" recommended plank width.

○   So we have to adjust the first row by trimming it down to add more planking width to the final row.

What we need to do to fix it:

Take the final rows measurement, which in our case is currently at 2 1/4".

Take a full plank width, which for us is 9".

Now we need to add the two measurements together, and then divide them in half.

Remember that whatever you take off the first row will be increasing the 2 1/4" end row strip.

So, 9"(full plank width) + 2.25 or 2 1/4"(current final row strip) = 11.25 or 11 1/4"(total together).

Now we need to figure out how much under the recommended 2 1/2" minimum plank width our final row would have been, which in our case was 2 1/4". So 1/4" under the recommended 2 1/2" plank width.

Take the 11.25 or 11 1/4" (total from before) and now deduct .25 or 1/4" from it(1/4 is how much under the minimum we were). Which now gives us 11".

Now I just divide 11 by 2(11/2 = 5.5) to get 5.5". So 5.5" is what I need to cut the first and last row to.

Let's double check to make sure our measurements are good:
- Room length = 13'.
- Convert 13' into inches: 13 x 12 = 156".
- Divide by 9" planking: 156 / 9 = 17.33.

- Take out a full plank (first row), and the .33 (last row) = 16 full planks.
- Now work out how many inches 16 planks are: 16(rows) x 9"(full plank widths) = 144".
- Add our new first and last row measurements of 5.5" together: 5.5 x 2 = 11".
- Now add the 11" to the 144": 11 = 144 = 155".

We now know that using a first and last plank row trimmed down to 5.5" and the remaining 16 full plank rows will measure 155". The room measures exactly 156" remember, but with two 3/8" expansion gaps at each end, the 155" allows for that and any other slight variations in the boards as we progress across our room.

I know this step takes a lot of working out. But the work done here could save you huge problems and issues at the end of the installation. If you want to put the flooring down right and make it look like a pro did it? Then take a few extra minutes working out your own measurements using the example above in your own rooms. Then you will be well on your way to a perfect install and a long-lasting laminate flooring.

Install The First Row(s) Of Laminate -

Let's Get Started!

First & Last Row Cuts Needed?

By now you will have worked out first and last row cuts(previous section - if needed), so it's time to cut the planks to size. Always make sure you cut the right end of the laminate before you start. You don't want to cut a plank and then realize you cut a tongue or groove off that you actually needed. And always cut from the top of the laminate to the bottom(depending on blade direction). If you are cutting a plank for the starting row you should remove the tongue edge. If you are cutting a plank for the end row you should remove the grooved side.

First & Last Row Cuts Not Needed?

If you will be using either full planks across the room, or have enough of a final plank to avoid having to cut both the first and last rows, we still need to do a little trimming!

To start the first row, trim off all the planks tongue edges(long side) that will be facing the wall from each of the planks in the first row. We do this to make sure we get a nice flush edge to push up against the spacers when we eventually slide them into place. With the cuts made, we can now get going on the first couple of rows.

LAYING THE FIRST PLANK:

We will start our very first row about two feet away from our starting wall with the grove end facing out across the room(tongue should already be trimmed off), and in a left-to-right direction across the room. We will also use a full plank to start(minus the tongue). The reason we are starting away from the wall is to give us space, and to make sure we start with a solid foundation to continue on with the rest of the rows. But don't worry, as soon as we are done with at least the first two rows of laminate, we will then slide them back against the wall making sure we don't forgot to put our expansion spacers in place first.

Now start to lay the first full plank down with the trimmed edge facing the starting wall. It's at this point that many first-time installers will just complete this first row only and then move on to the next, and then go row by row after that. But in order to make sure we give ourselves a solid foundation and a nice solid base to build from, we will be installing the first plank of the second row next(pictured below).

First two boards placed down away from starting wall.

Before we start on the second row, and in fact every other row from here on. You should keep in-mind a few things first.

○   Always keep the 3/8" expansion gap around the perimeter at the walls.

○   First plank of any row must be at least 8" long.

○   Offset all end joints by at least 12".

○   Remember to use cuts from previous rows to start new rows if you can.

When you start on the first plank in the second row(2), because you started two feet away from the wall you can actually kneel on the first row as you insert the second. Doing this will not only keep everything secure, but it will also make sure nothing moves as you try to connect one plank to another, especially if you need to use the tapping block or pull bar.

Another thing to note at this point. When you move further away from the starting point, and as you start to install more planks in the first two rows you can place a box of flooring or something heavy at the opposite end from you(your starting point). This will make sure that as you move down the row to the other end, the boards where you started are not moving all over the place or disconnecting from one another.

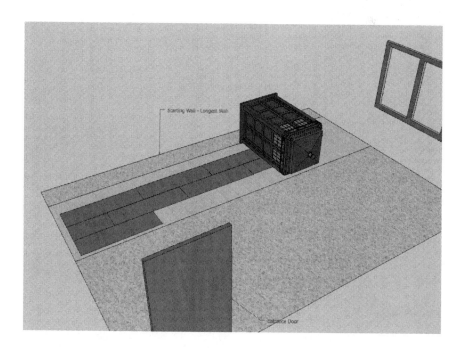

Heavy object at opposite end to stop rows moving! ;-)

FIRST PLANK SECOND ROW:

For the second row, we want to cut down this plank so we can stagger the end seams at least 12" across joining rows over the entire floor. So depending on the length of your own flooring planks, you want to make sure the first and second row end joints are greater than 12" apart. Here is a little cheat that may help you with your flooring stagger patterns.

Joint Distances:

You can either do this randomly by making sure you always keep that 12" stagger between the previous or next rows end joints. Or you can follow the measurements below instead.

1/2 Plank Stagger Pattern: (Always start first row, first plank, using a full plank):

For a full 48" starting laminate board length: Cut next row to 24" - Row after that would be a full plank, then next row 24", and so on.

For a full 36" board length: Cut next row to 18" - Row after would be full, then 18", then full.

This pattern is simple to do, but can look a bit generic and too uniform to be honest. Also make sure you check the flooring directions to see if this stagger pattern is permitted.

Half Plank Stagger Pattern.

Stagger Pattern Of Thirds:
My personal favorite, and here's how it works.

Full – 2/3 – 1/3 - Plank Stagger Pattern: (Always start first row, first plank, using a full plank)
48" First board length: Cut next row to 36", next row after that to 16", then back to full plank(48")
36" First board length: Cut next row to 24", next row after that to 12", then back to full plank(36")

I love the look of the pattern of thirds the most! It looks much more pleasing to the eye, and more like a real hardwood than the 1/2 stagger pattern. Always remember the 12" minimum end joint recommendation, especially if your flooring is less than 36" long.

Stagger of Thirds Plank Pattern.

When you select your stagger pattern and cut the first plank in the second row to the desired length, it's now time to install it.

Clicking the planks together.

Hold the second plank at a slight angle as you bring the tongue and groove closer together, then gently click the two planks together with a slight downward pressure making sure there are no gaps in the seams. If you do see a slight gap, then just take the tapping block and lightly tap the two together until the seam disappears. With that first plank in the second row down, we can now move on with the next plank. Here is what your first two planks should look like to this point if you want to follow along.

Plank 1 down - Plank 2 down.

For the third plank, we will add a second plank back in the first row. So we will be using another one of our tongue-trimmed planks we cut specifically for the first row.

THIRD PLANK BACK IN FIRST ROW:

Grab another full plank with the tongue trimmed off, and at a slight angle insert it into the end of the first plank in the first row(1), then lightly click the two ends together with a slight downward pressure. If you find you have any gaps at the joining seams, just use your tapping block and lightly tap the two ends together.

FOURTH PLANK BACK IN SECOND ROW:

Before we go any further, I just want to calm your fears and let you know that I will not be covering each and every plank in your installation. Can you imagine how big this guide would be if I did? All I'm doing is breaking down the first and most critical part of your install, as well as showing you the pattern and order we will be laying our planks in, just to give us a solid foundation to build from.

I'm going to provide you with an image so that you can see the best order to lay your planks in, and then you can just go off by yourself and install the rest of your floor if you like. But I will be stopping at other critical points during this install to let you know of any hazards to avoid, or tricks you can use to make this laminate flooring install even easier. But for now, it's time to put down your fourth plank in the second row.

For the fourth plank you will be using a full un-trimmed plank(4). This is because you should have already cut the first plank in that row depending on your layout pattern(1/2 Stagger or 1/3 Stagger). Pretty easy from here huh? Well, actually it will be the first plank you will be laying where you have to bring two meeting seams together, one on the long side, and one on the end(4). So it can be a little tricky actually.

Laying The 4ᵗʰ Plank Down.

The trick to this plank is to insert the long side of plank 4 into the first row of plank 1 and 3, all while getting the end of plank 4 as close to the first plank in the second row, plank 2, as possible. But still leaving a little gap so that I can bring the ends together after, using my tapping block.

Some newer laminate flooring tongue and groove systems actually do not need to be held at an angle anymore to insert them into the other planks. This means that you basically just press down on the seams and they click together. But I am assuming you are using the style of tongue and groove flooring that needs to be placed into position at a slight angle, and then clicked into place. Which means that you cannot attach two sides at the same time.

So for our fourth plank, let's start as I outlined above by now placing it into the groove of the first row(1)(3) planks, and close enough to the first plank(2) in that row, just so you have a tiny bit of space between the end of this plank and the end of the first plank(pictured below). Now click(press) the long side of this plank down.

Leaving a small gap at the end so I can tap the long ends together

With the long side of plank 4 in place and a little gap

remaining at the end, we now need to grab our tapping block and lightly tap the two long ends together. As you tap from the opposite end of the gap on plank 4, notice the gap you left at the other end start to close up and connect together and interlock with the first plank in that row(2).

Remember to not over-tap the two planks because you don't want to damage the seams, or knock the boards too far and out of line with each other. If you do, just lightly tap the other end back into position with your tapping block, because at this point we still have space to access this side of the row. However, if you come up against this problem when you are almost done with the first two rows, you will have to use your pull-bar because of the space restriction. Told you these tools would come in handy! ;)

Now we have our first four planks installed, carry on with the rest of the first two rows using the techniques we have already discussed, and the picture of order below. Next, we will cover placing the two final planks on each end of the first two rows.

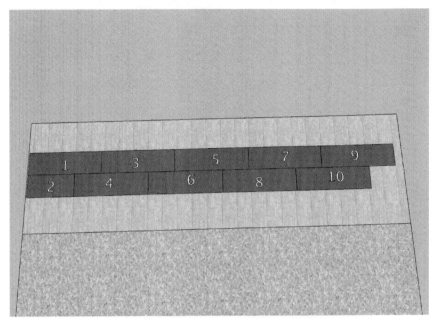

Picture of order - First two rows

FINAL PLANKS - FIRST TWO ROWS:

By now you should be at the last two planks in the first two rows of your laminate install(pictured above). As you probably can see by now, it really is pretty simple to do this yourself huh? So, well done getting to this point!

With only two more planks left to complete the first two rows, it's now time to slide the flooring back against the starting wall, but make sure you put all the expansion spacers in place first. Many installers do this step when they have both the first two rows completed. But I like to do it before, just in case the wall is not very square, and you may find that when you slide the completed rows back your expansion gap disappears because of an uneven wall at each end of the room. Whereas sliding the two rows back now with the two final planks still left to cut and place, we can be sure we are cutting exactly what we need off the final two planks in those rows.

So right now we will slide our first two rows back against that starting wall, and our expansion spacers(pictured below).

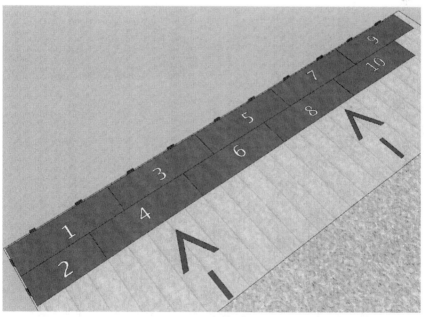

Pushing first two rows back against the starting wall. Remember the spacers!

Let's put down the last plank in the first row. Again, for this row we will be using one of the trimmed planks you cut down already for the first row at the beginning of your install. In most cases we will also have to cut down this last plank at the end, just to make sure it fits our room, and includes enough space for our expansion gap. If you do not need to cut it, and you have enough of an expansion gap at the end, then you just need to place a full plank down without any adjustments.

For those of you that do need to cut that last plank, here are a few easy steps..

1) Measure from the end of the previous plank in that row to the wall. Remember you want to measure from the top of your laminate flooring, and not from the groove. Write down this measurement.

2) Subtract the 3/8"(or whatever expansion gap your flooring calls for) from that measurement.

3) Now mark the plank you will be cutting so you know exactly how much to cut off.

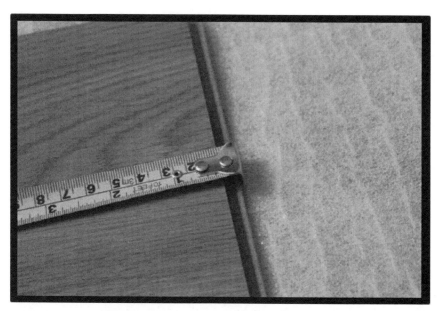

Do not measure from the groove.

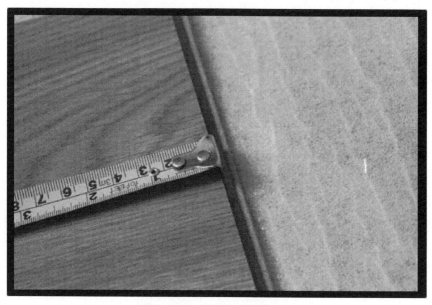

Measure from the top.

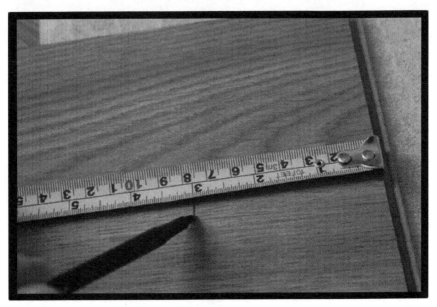

Mark, and then make your cuts.

4) Cut the plank to size making sure you chop off the right side of the plank. ;)

5) With the plank now cut to size, place down the spacers on the end wall, and then proceed to install the last plank in that row, as you have previously done with the others.

You should have plenty of room to hold this plank(11) at an angle and install it flush with the previous plank(9). However, if you do find that you have a small gap in between the end seams, just use your pull-bar to tap them tight together, because you will not have the space at this point to use your tapping block. Please be gentle and tap very lightly to secure them together.

LAST PLANK OF SECOND ROW:

For this plank(12), you will pretty much be following the same steps as the previous paragraph. Again, make sure you keep that expansion gap in mind when you cut that final plank to size, and also place a spacer down at the end to make sure it's the perfect fit. So go ahead and install the last plank of the first two rows.

Two Rows Completed.

Congratulations! The first two rows are now complete, and you should have a perfect foundation to carry on with the rest of your installation across the room. Make sure to follow the correct plank order as you progress with the install(pictured below), and always keep that expansion gap around the perimeter at all times.

If you decided on a stagger pattern at the beginning of this chapter, then cutting the rest of the planks should be pretty straight-forward. But if you decided on your own stagger pattern, then please just make sure you follow your flooring directions in order to keep staggering the end seams to what they recommend.

USE THE WASTE! HEADS UP:

From the third row on you should start to use some of the cut pieces from the previous rows. Obviously, you trimmed the first row down so you cannot use these planks. But every time you need to start a row from this point on, see if you can use a cut plank from a previous row to either start a new one, or end on one. This will cut down so much on your waste! Many first-time installers overlook this option, and just keep grabbing new planks from the package to cut from! Such a WASTE!

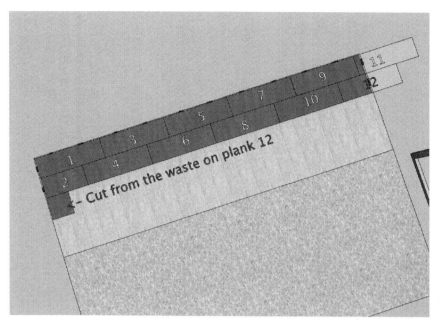

Cut from the waste on plank 12

Using the waste from previous rows to start a new one

PLANK ORDER:

I'm now going to show you what order to lay down the planks in, right up until you almost get to the end of the first row of underlayment. Of course your own flooring may be different and the numbers may vary. But at least this highlights the correct pattern of order to carry on installing your own planks in.

Order pattern for the first few rows

When we get to the point where we are a few inches away from the end of our first row of underlayment(pictured above), it's time to place down a second row. The reason we want to leave a few inches of space and not just install the planks right to the edge, is because some laminate underlayment requires an overlap between rows. So we don't want to cover this space up just yet.

Grab another row of underlayment and lay it down however it is recommended in the directions. Usually this means a few inches of overlap, and pulling off the peel and stick self-adhesive strip before sticking them together. But whatever way you need to do it, we can now place another row down.

Laying down another row of underlayment.

With a second row of underlayment placed down, just keep following the order you have already been using to install the rest of your laminate flooring. And place more rows of underlayment down as needed. When you get to the last couple of rows, come back to this guide, and we will move on from there.

In the next section we will cover our final rows of planking to make sure we finish the install the right way.

FINAL ROWS OF THE INSTALL

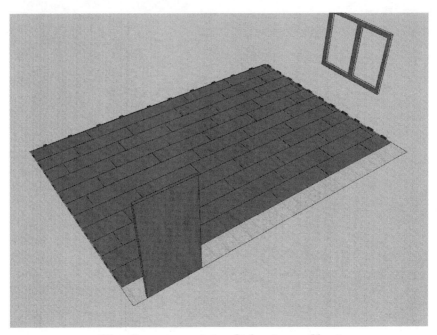

The last row(s) of the installation

We are now at the final rows of our laminate flooring installation, so pat yourself on the back. It is at this point of the install when you usually have to do some more cutting, adjusting, and just general tinkering in order to get that last row to fit. Depending on how you have been installing your laminate flooring, you may also find that you will have to change the direction you face while laying the planks down, because you will be coming up to the finishing wall, and do not have enough space to install the flooring kneeling in the direction you have been.

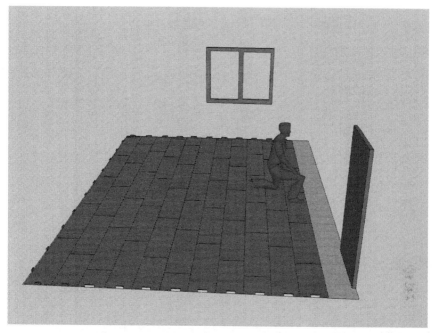

A change of direction could be needed.

THE FINAL ROW(S) OF OUR INSTALLATION:

If you have been following this guide from the start of this chapter, you should already know what you have to cut this final row down to? Or maybe you got lucky and didn't even need to cut this last row down at all. Whatever the scenario, this final row can be a little tricky for some, especially if you are ending by a doorway or something similar?

For the last row against a flat wall, all you need to do is double-check your measurements to make sure you have the correct final plank width. Of course nothing is 100%, so you may have to take off a little more or a little less than previously thought, but it should not be a huge difference at all. Simply cut each plank down one at a time making sure you measure for each individual plank. I do this because sometimes you will find the end wall is not 100% square. So it's not a good idea to cut the entire row all at once like we did with the first row, and then find that you are too close to the wall on one end. This would mean that you may have to make another cut to a couple of extra planks. So go one-by-one in this last row.

When you have cut the first plank in the last row, go ahead and click it into position and place a spacer behind it. You may need to use a pull-bar here to join any gaps together, even on the long side of the plank, because you will not have enough space to use a tapping block. But for each one of the final row of planks, follow the steps above to complete your installation!

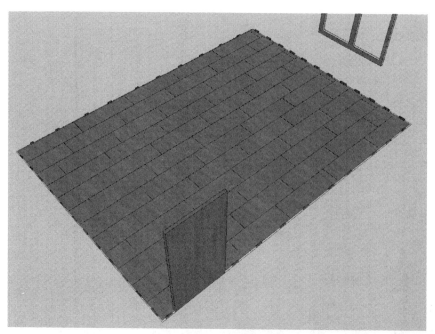

The perfect world! Completed laminate flooring install!

DOORWAYS:

Arrggghhhhh! It's a doorway! Ok, I made the room in the picture above end near a doorway for a reason. And this section is for those of you that might face a struggle when installing laminate flooring against a doorway.

Most of the time when installing laminate flooring you will find that you usually end near a doorway, which is why I put the section here. But it doesn't really matter where you come up against a doorway, because they can usually always be a little tricky, especially for the first-time installer!

Here is a picture of what I'm talking about!...

Problem area next to a doorway.

As you can see, you don't have a lot of room, and you usually cannot hold a plank at the angle needed to click it into place with the previous rows planks, because of the door moulding. So what do you do?

Here are a few steps to help you on your way to installing a plank under a doorway. Obviously I'm assuming that you followed the "Prepping" section and have already undercut the moulding around the door? If not, now would be a good time to do it.

Always keep the expansion gap, even if meeting

up against the other flooring from another room. And remember that you may want to leave a little extra space to allow for transition strip channels to be placed between the two floors. ##

METHOD ONE:

1) Measure the distance from the wall to the previous row of laminate. Remember the expansion gap!

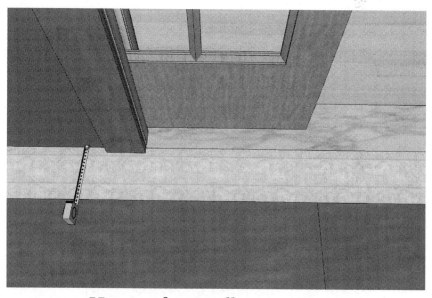

Measure from wall to previous row.

2) Subtract the expansion gap and make a note of the distance.

3) Cut the final rows plank to the correct width.

4) Take the plank and slide the cut side first under the cut door moulding.

Placing the plank under the door moulding, at an angle.

5) Now slide the plank back toward the previous row and get the two longest seams as close as you can together, almost as though the last plank is resting on the other one. Just like in the picture below.

Getting the two seams as close as I can before I tap them into place.

6) Now take a pull-bar and gently tap the two seams together. You may have to put a little downward pressure on the plank you are installing to make sure the tongue connects with the groove securely. Please make sure to start tapping lightly, taking care not to chip any of the finish off either plank.

As I start to tap, the two seams will come together.

7) With the two longest sides of the row connected,

you will now need to use a pull-bar to connect the end of this plank into the previous plank of this row(pictured below). If you have space here you can also use the tapping block.

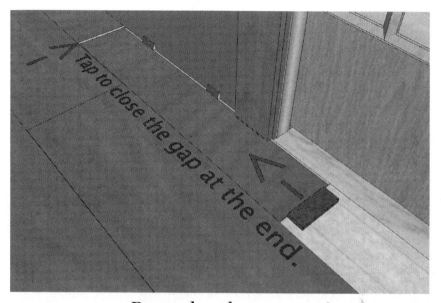

Tap to close the gap at the end.

Remember those spacers!

8) Now tap together the two ends until all meeting edges are tight with no visible gaps.

Now you just repeat this process for the other door moulding.

METHOD TWO:

If for some reason you cannot undercut the door moulding or remove it, you may need an extra tool to help you in this case. Because we cannot go under the moulding we need to trace around it using a contour-gauge. You can pick one up from your local hardware store. This tool allows us to basically trace the shape of the door moulding, and then apply it to our plank.

1) Push the contour-gauge with firm pressure up against the door moulding so it traces the shape.

2) Now place the contour-gauge on top of the plank you will be cutting, directly where it will come into contact with the moulding.

3) Trace the shape out using a pen directly onto the laminate plank.

4) Now you need to add the 3/8" expansion gap around your previous trace marks. I usually eye-ball this and replicate the shape from step #1.

5) Cut with a jigsaw to get the most accurate cut possible.

6) Place the plank down and install it into position using a pull-bar or tapping block.

7) Because you cannot take the moulding off, the expansion gap will be visible at this location. So the best thing to do is to fill the void with a colored

caulking to hide the gap from view.

END OF THE INSTALL, CONGRATULATIONS!

You have just completed your laminate flooring installation, and possibly saved yourself thousands! It's a great feeling to complete your first one. And I hope it empowers you to do many more floors in the future. Well done!

To finish off your installation you should always go over the room and inspect your work. Check the expansion gaps, and look for anything else that may stand out to you. If you are happy and everything looks fine, then just remove all the spacers from around the room and cut away any excess or visible vapor barrier and underlayment. Now let the flooring do its thing! A good old sweep never hurts at this point either.

Even though the flooring is complete, we still need to put back the moulding, and possibly add some transition strips to the joining rooms. So this is what we will cover in the next section.

The Installation - Step #3 - Install The Moulding

It must be a great feeling to have just installed your own laminate flooring. Now we need to finish off the install with some moulding to cover the expansion gap.

You may have previously removed your old moulding in order to reuse it here? Or you may have purchased some new moulding or quarter rounds at the same time as your flooring? Whatever the case may be, we now need to install them around the perimeter of our rooms.

Moulding - Qtr Rounds:

This part of the install itself is pretty easy because it usually means just cutting the moulding to size, making the correct bevel for the corners, and then installing it. But here are a few things to keep in mind while you do it.

- Never nail or glue any moulding to the floor!
- Always nail or glue to the wall.

The purpose of a free-floating floor is to keep it,

"free-floating" so it can expand and contract without any restrictions. If you nail or glue the moulding to the floor, when it does move it will either buckle the flooring, or just pull the moulding away from the walls!

- ○ Never install the moulding too tight against the floor to restrict its movement.

You may not nail or glue the moulding into the laminate flooring, but you can still install them so tight to the floor that it restricts its movement. This again can cause it to buckle or damage the moulding, or in some cases scratch the floor because of the two surfaces rubbing together around the perimeter. Just install the moulding lightly touching the floor giving it ample opportunity to move without any issues at all. You don't need to leave a gap here. I'm just saying to allow the moulding to sit on the floor and not press down on it.

If at some point in the installation you didn't worry too much about getting the expansion gap 100% correct, and just left it slightly bigger in some areas. You may find that you can still see a gap between the flooring and the moulding, even when you put it up against the wall. If this happens in your room, you can either pad out behind the moulding with some thin wood before you nail it to the wall, then cover the small gap at the top of the moulding with caulking when you are done. Or, if you are using regular base moulding, you can always buy a quarter round moulding and attach them together like in the pictures below. This will give you an extra 3/4" of moulding around the perimeter, and cover that extra gap.

Base moulding only.

Base moulding and quarter round together.

Whichever moulding method you decide is up to you. As long as you cover the gap and give the flooring freedom to move, this step of the install should be pretty simple.

Transition Strips:

Meeting up to other rooms by doorways, or in sections that span two rooms may bring up all kinds of worries and issues. But don't get too overwhelmed with what to do at this point, because you have a bunch of easy options when installing a transition strip.

Depending on what flooring you are meeting up against with your laminate, you may need a different profile of transition strip. You may also need to allow a little extra gap between the two rooms when you install the laminate flooring. This is because some transition strips come with a channel that you just snap them into. So you have to allow space for this channel, and also compensate for the expansion gap as well.

Visit you local hardware store and take a look at the various transition strips on offer. You will see some for laminate flooring to tile, laminate to carpet, laminate to sheet vinyl, and even laminate to laminate transitions. Everything is pretty much covered with a matching transition piece. And many times it's just up to what style you want. But here are a few important things to keep in mind when purchasing and installing transition strips.

Never nail or glue them to the laminate flooring - Even with transition strips you must keep the laminate free-floating.

- ○ Always keep the expansion gap when installing moulding & transitions.
- ○ Measure the height of both floors before you visit the store to make sure the transition can accept both of them.
- ○ Always ask an associate if the transition is acceptable with laminate flooring.
- ○ And of course…..measure the width of the area

you will need to transition over! ;)

You have many options available to you when selecting a transition piece. So take your time, ask, and make sure you get the correct one. Sometimes color choices are what will hold you up the most, as many of the local stores will have wood colored versions, white ones, almond ones, and plain ones that you can paint or stain. But when in doubt, you can always go with the standard silver or gold transition strips. Bit boring I know, but gets the job done.

The Installation - Additional Layouts Explained

We have already tackled the layout and installation for a pretty basic square/rectangle room. But I just wanted to quickly cover an additional section, just for those of you with a slightly different layout than we discussed in our installation chapter.

As I already went in-depth over the installation process, I'll try to keep this section as brief as possible. You can still follow the exact same steps to lay the planks down. But I feel it's important to quickly go over a common problem those of you may have if your room resembles the layout below.

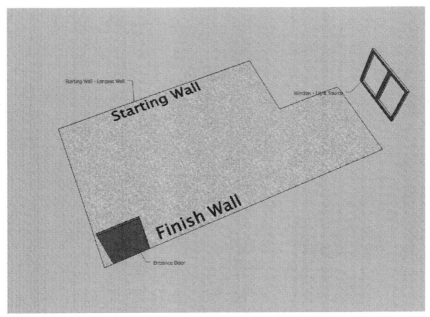

A common additional layout plan.

As you can see we have a slight modification to our standard square room. And many of you would think, so what? In most cases you can pretty much tackle this the same way as any other install and be fine. But, you are taking a chance that when you hit that jog-out section(right-side pictured above) of the room, you may have a few issues if you don't plan for it ahead of time.

The main problem a room like this can bring, is when you hit the corner problem area below.

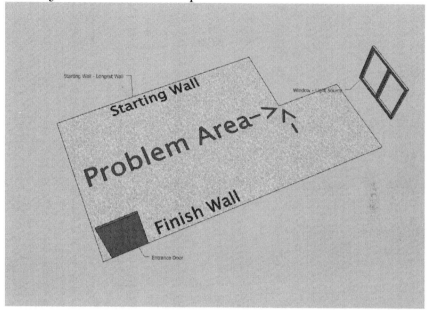

This section could be a problem if not dealt with sooner.

Up until this point everything may have been pretty smooth with your install. But if you hit this problem area, you will probably need to cut out a chunk from a plank, which may be no big deal? But what if the cut you need to make is too thin for the plank? Remember that you really don't want to have to cut a slither of planking to less than 2 1/2" wide. So if you didn't plan ahead for this and need to cut below that measurement, then you could be in trouble.

The Remedy:

Here is a simple way to avoid any issues in a room with a layout like the one above. If you take just a few extra steps you will not need to worry about any layout issues along the way. So follow along as I try to make this as seamless as possible.

If you followed along from the start of "The Install" section, you should already know how many planks you will use to get from one side of your room, to the other. If you didn't go over this section yet, I recommend you do before we continue any further. Because you will need to know how many planks it will take to cross your room.

In the case of the new layout above, what we will basically be doing is taking two measurements across our room. One from the starting wall to the end wall(already done in The Install section). And the other from the starting wall to our problem point where the room extends out(pictured below).

Step 1) Measure from starting wall to the problem area(outside corner - pictured below).

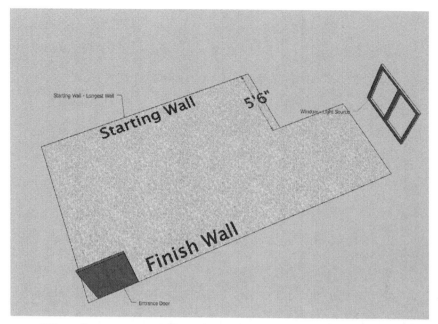

Five feet, six inches from the starting wall to the outside corner edge.

Step 2) Divide the measurement from step#1 by the width of your plank.

My example: 5.5 x 12(to convert 5 feet 6 into inches) = 66"

*For calculations sake, remember that half of 12"(one foot) is 6". But when using a calculator I had to use .5 to represent 6", just to get the right numbers in my calculator. That's why you see 5.5 above and not 5.6.

Now I divide 66(step1) by 9(plank width) as outlined in step 2 to to get: **7.33 planks.** (66 / 9 = 7.33)

So, I'm looking at 7 full planks and .33(3rd) of another to get to that outside corner. And we pretty much know that a third of my 9" plank is about a 3" strip, which would be fine to cut for this room and also over the 2 1/2" plank width minimum. Even when I deduct my 3/8" expansion gap I'm still over it. I can now just carry on my way knowing that I will not have any issues when I get to that problem area of my room.

Now what if I'm not starting my install with a full plank width? Maybe I had to trim this first row to allow the last row to be over the minimum width requirement? Or, when I completed the two previous steps, I would be left with a plank that was under the 2 1/2" minimum? Then go to step #3!

Step 3) Go to, "Math Haters Unite!" ;-)

The Installation - Math Haters Unite

On one install job I did, it was late in the day and I needed to just get it done. But for some reason I could not face planning all the cut sizes and layouts out in-advanced. I guess it was just one of those days for me, and I needed a quick method to work out all my cuts without having to take out my calculator!

After a quick brainstorm I came up with an idea that was super-quick, minimal waste, and would give me my cut sizes in a matter of minutes! Here is what I did!…

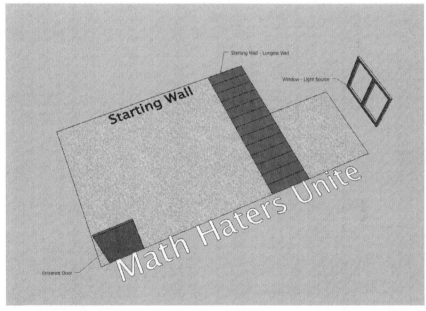

A time-saving, calculator-free measuring method.

* **Remember to use your expansion gap spacers, even when using this method.***

All I did was lay an entire single row of planks from my starting wall to the end wall as in the picture above. I started as usual by trimming off the tongue from the first plank only, inserting my spacers, and from there I just inserted the other planks until I got to the other side of the room (finish wall).

When you use this method for a regular square room, you will quickly be able to work out if you need to cut the first and last row of planks in order to avoid having to cut anything under the 2 1/2" minimum plank width. And in most cases, you only need to take a little off the final row to get what you need.

If you encounter a room with a similar shape to the picture above, but maybe with a few alterations to it? You can still use this highly adaptable method for those locations. Just lay down a row of planks from one wall to the other, place the row right next to the outside corner or problem area, and it will give you a great view of how much you will need to cut from the starting row, or the end row. And also show you where the middle rows line up against a problem area. Hopefully you won't have to make any cuts at all? But that is usually not the case.

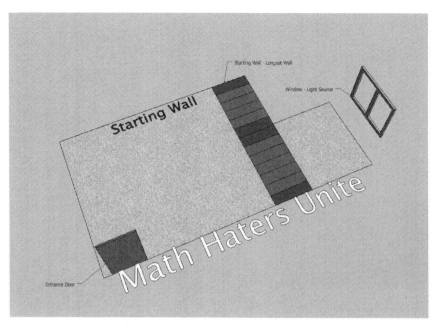

Starting Wall

Starting Wall - Longest Wall

Window - Light Source

Entrance Door

Math Haters Unite

Red planks represent possible areas of adjustment, and problem spots.

When your row is complete, take a look at the outside corner section to see what may need to be adjusted at that point.

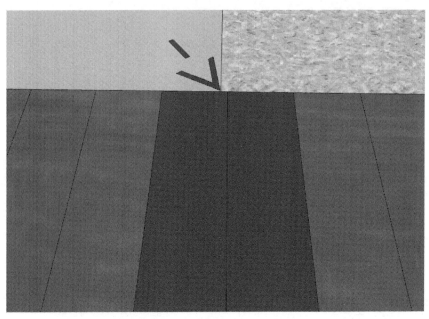

Close-up of the outside corner of our layout.

I've made the important planks red in this image to highlight the planks we need to focus on here. As you can see we have a small section of plank overlapping the corner(red arrow). So we need to check this measurement to make sure it's over the 2 1/2" plank width minimum.

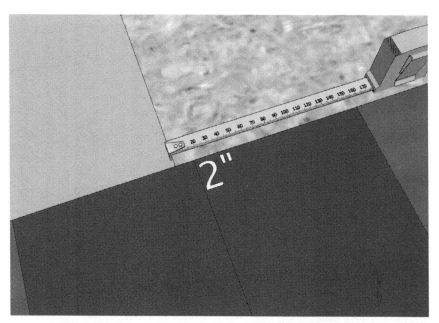

A 2" plank row would be under the minimum. I also included the 3/8" expansion gap into this measurement.

If you find as we have in the picture above, that you need to adjust this section of planking. We then need to look at the last row to see how much we may need to cut off. We look at the final row before the first row because we will always want to start the first row with a full plank width if we can.

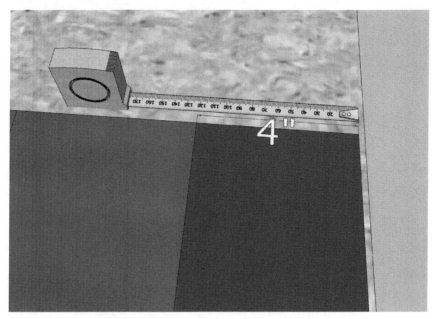

A 4" final plank row would need to be adjusted to fit the middle section.

In our example we are looking at a 4" plank width in our last row. But we also know we need to adjust this a little to compensate for the 2" plank width in the middle row that was under the minimum requirement. In order to do this we need to take some off the very first row of planks against our starting wall.

What do we know at this point?

○ We now know we need to adjust the middle section by at least 1/2" one way. Or about 2" the other.

○ We also know that our last row width of 4" is over the minimum.

○ And we know that we used a full widths plank at the start of our row.

So to begin our adjustments, the easiest way to do this is to adjust the very first row of planking. We actually have enough plank width in that first row to line up the middle section, so we may not need to cut any planks around this corner at all.

If I trim just 2" off my first row of planking, it will move everything back toward the starting wall by the same amount, line up the middle rows by the problem corner, and still leaves me a nice 6" width of plank in that last row.

This simple adjustment has lined everything up, and kept all the planks over the minimum plank width. It means that I can now use full planks around that problem outside corner, without having to worry about it.

Here are my final measurements.

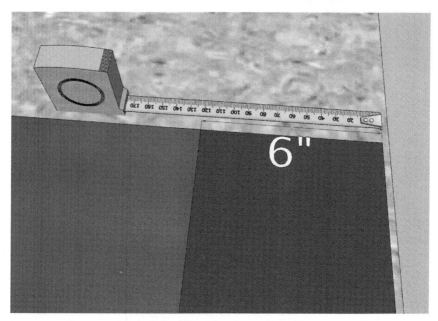

Final row is now 6".

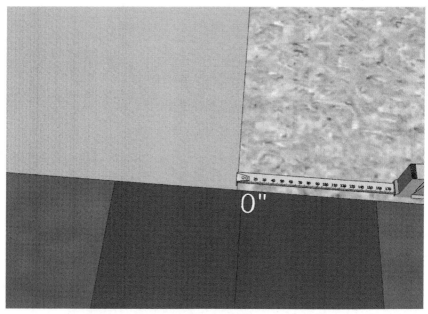

Middle row now does not need to be cut.

Notice the small expansion gap in the picture? I

compensated for it in my measurements around that corner.

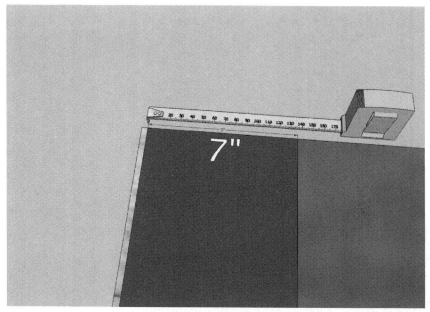

First row trimmed down by 2" to allow adjustments in other rows.

Hopefully you see the benefit of using the "Math Haters Unite" method. It's just so simple to do and takes much less time than the previous traditional methods. But of course traditional methods are always extremely accurate as well, and they also allow you to plan the cuts before you even enter a room or job-site.

Whichever method you pick to figure out your room, just make sure you measure twice, and cut once. And as always, make sure to allow for the expansion gaps.

This concludes The Installation section of this guide. But it's still not entirely done. In the next section I will cover things to keep in-mind after the install is finished.

After The Install

After the install is complete and everything is ready to go back into the room, you might want to take a few minutes to read over this next short section called, "After The Install". I just wanted to add a chapter that gives you some great tips on how to keep your laminate flooring looking great. And also how to keep any problems that may occur to a minimum.

Sections covered in this chapter are:
- The Clean Up
- Floor Protection

After The Install - The Clean Up

To clean up after the install, and in fact throughout the life of the laminate flooring you should purchase a good flooring cleaner. Most people will just vacuum and wash with generic floor cleaners and I can't tell them not too enough! If you use too much solution or water, you could end up destroying the floor you worked so hard to install!

When you visit your local hardware store you will no doubt be presented with vast amounts of flooring cleaners. Many of the cleaners are usually a multipurpose type of cleaner that claims to do it all, no matter what type of flooring you have. But I always direct people away from the generic cleaners and instead show them the brands that are specifically for laminate floors. And the reason I do this is because a lot of the generic cleaners will leave a slight film on top of the finish, which can be a real pain to get rid of. And you may also find that if anything happens to the flooring finish, when you call the manufacturer to assist, the first thing they will ask is, "What did you use to clean it with?" Using a bad cleaner can actually void your warranty!

Whenever you buy a new laminate flooring, it's always a good idea to call the manufacturer to see what cleaners they recommend you use. Pergo and Bruce Flooring actually have their own branded laminate flooring cleaners, and as you can guess they work really well. Most of the laminate flooring manufacturers will suggest you use one of their own branded products for laminate floors. Zep is another brand of cleaners that offer a laminate only product, and I've heard good things about it, but have never personally used it. What can I say? I'm a big fan of the Pergo and Bruce cleaners! ;)

You will find that in most cases the laminate flooring cleaners are actually in a spray bottle, so that you can deliver a thin spray only and not saturate the floor, which would be bad. The best way to use the cleaners is to lightly spray over a 4' x 4' area, and then wipe over with a decent microfiber mop before moving on to the next section of your floor. You should never apply any type of laminate cleaner with a wet mop, as this can really do a job on your flooring over time. Just read the directions on the back of the cleaner, and you will be well on your way to making the floor look as good as new.

After The Install - Floor Protection

Yes, laminate flooring is extremely tough! But it's by no means indestructible. And nobody should ever tell you it is. No matter what type of flooring you buy, if you hit it right, with the right thing, and at the right angle, it's going to scratch. So here are a few things you can buy to make sure you are taking good precautions to prevent any damage to your floors.

Furniture Casters / Pads:

Relatively inexpensive furniture casters could save you many headaches, and your flooring a lot of scratches. These kinds of products simply stick or nail into the bottom feet of chairs, tables, refrigerators, ovens, and anything else that if moved could cause all kinds of problems. I always recommend casters to all my customers, because I've seen some awful problems caused to the finish on a laminate that could have been avoided for under a $10 cost! It's just not worth it!

Silicone / Caulk:

When installing laminate in kitchens or in bathrooms where water is prevalent, you should always protect your flooring from any spills. And usually the best way to do this is to use some caulking sealant in the expansion gap around areas like the tub, kitchen sink, and dish washer. Some installers even use a thin bead all the way around the perimeter in those areas. The good thing about caulking is that it still stays flexible, even when dry. This allows your laminate flooring to move freely, and still be protected and sealed. But check with your manufacturer for recommendations of course.

Doctor Laminate

Over the years in the laminate installing and sales business, you get to pick up some really great tips while on the job. I've also received some awesome advice from other long-term laminate installers that I want to share with you here. So just in case you ever come up against one of these situations with your own laminate flooring, you can always come back to this chapter.

Sections covered in this chapter are:
- Dents & Scratches
- Lifting Floor?
- Replacing A Plank

Doctor Laminate - Dents & Scratches

The first one is always the worst! ;-)

Another common question I get is how to take care of a scratch or dent in the floor. You didn't mean to do it, but you came home and dropped something on that perfect laminate flooring, and it chips! I know, because

I've done it myself. So here are a few things that could help you to make it look as good as new again.

Putty - Filler:

Pergo, Bruce, and many other laminate flooring companies offer color coordinated putty and fillers just for this reason. If you dent your floor or get a deep scratch, a colored putty could be the solution. Usually they come in very small tubes that you match to the color of the floor. Then you just snip off the end and apply to the damaged area, while smoothing over with your finger when you are done. Let it harden for a few hours without anyone walking on it, and you should be left with a hard finish that blends in with the rest of the floor.

Most putty and fillers are a matte finish when dry. So if you have a gloss flooring finish, you may not get the look you wanted using a putty.

Colored Wax Pens:

You may have seen them already in the laminate flooring aisle right next to the floors? They look like regular crayons and feel like a wax of some sort. They are actually really similar to a putty that you apply by basically rubbing them over the scratch, which leaves a thin film that hopefully covers the damaged area. The pens are really only good for surface scratches and light dents, but I've still had some good results while using them. The only downside is the amount of colors available being only a light, medium, or dark selection. So you sometimes have to try to get one that's as close to your flooring as possible.

Furniture Pens:

Not my first choice, but many installers use them on light surface scratches and claim they work great! You will usually find them in a paint store or somewhere that sells stains and polyurethane products. The pens are around $5-$10 each. They work great on furniture and may work well on a laminate flooring away from the heavy traffic areas. But if the damage is right in the middle of the floor, you might want to try one of the previous options first.

Re-finishers / Polyurethane:

A couple of my installer friends use products like Rejuvenate, or Orange Glow to restore older laminate flooring finishes. And they really do look good when they are done. You have to understand though that these products will need to be applied every few months, depending on how much foot traffic your room gets. So it really is a temporary solution. However newer laminate re-finishers come with a polyurethane base that does a good job protecting your floors.

Of course I would only recommend re-finishers for older laminate floors where the finish has worn down. And also only when your warranty has long expired. But they are products that a home owner can do without any need for expensive tools, and with very little knowledge needed.

Doctor Laminate - Lifting Floor - Ripples - Buckles - Cupping

Cupping signs in flooring

One of the downsides of laminate flooring is actually

also a positive! Laminate is always touted as one of the most simple to install, no glue, no nails, and it simply just clicks together and your done. So many first-time installers do not even read the directions, and then just go ahead full-steam and install their floors without using any expansion gap at all. Or, many of you may have moved into a home that already has a laminate flooring installed, and are starting to see parts of the floor buckling or lifting up in certain areas around the room?

About 95% of the problem when you start to notice a laminate lifting or rippling, is because of an expansion gap being not big enough, or not there at all? So what do you do if you start to notice this in your own homes? First, do not panic! If you caught it early enough you can fix it without any long-term damage to the flooring. And second, it's not actually that hard to fix in most cases.

Notice the ripples in this floor?

Confirm The Problem - And Find The Location:
The first step would be to actually confirm that the expansion gap(if there is one) is the problem in the first place? It could also be a nail through the flooring, or maybe the moulding is too tight against the floor for it to move freely? A good point to start would be to inspect the flooring gap near the area that the problem is the most visible. So locate any doors in the room near that area, because the flooring is usually more assessable under a door than it is under the moulding. You may have to remove a transition strip to uncover the expansion gap. But I'd still rather have to get a new $5 transition strip than have to replace a laminate flooring worth thousands! Even if the door is nowhere near the problem area, it's still a good idea to investigate

it anyway.

After you remove the doorway transition strip the expansion gap should now be exposed. You will probably notice no gap at all(pictured below), or a perfectly spaced expansion gap all the way across. If you see a reduced expansion gap in that area this could still be perfectly normal, because the flooring may have expanded into it as it's designed to do. But it should not be touching too tightly up against another surface.

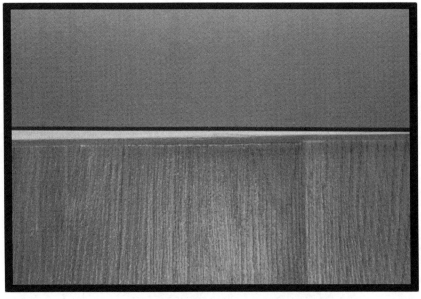

Uh oh! No expansion gap!

If you find yourself without an expansion gap around your floors, then we need to fix this as soon as possible to prevent any long-lasting damage. But if you find that your expansion gap is fine in that particular area, you need to check other areas around the room. And this usually means lifting off baseboard moulding near where the affected area is most visible. If your floor is showing visible signs of buckling or lifting, somewhere in that room you will find that your flooring is being restricted from moving as it should.

Sometimes as you start to take off moulding around the room, you may notice the buckling and lifting greatly diminish. This is usually a sign that it was the moulding causing the problem. But this is a good thing however, because it just means that once you've checked the expansion gap is good, all you have to do is put all the moulding back on, but just not as tight against the flooring as it was before.

If you get into the situation when you have removed all the moulding and the flooring is still buckling and lifting, you will now need to start visibly checking the entire perimeter for any areas where the flooring is tight up against the walls. At this point, also look for nail heads through the floor, screws, or anything that could be blocking the expansion gap. When you see a trouble spot or area that is pressing up against the wall, follow the next few steps to correct the problem.

Problem Area Located:

Step 1) Find the problem area in the room. Then go over to the opposite side and measure the other gap in the flooring by that wall. If you don't find a gap there, then jump right to step#3.

Step 2) Once you have measured the gap on the opposite wall, you should divide that measurement by two in order to get an approximate idea on what the expansion gap was. Obviously, as all the laminate planks will expand and constrict, this measurement will not be 100% accurate. But it will give you a good idea to start with. And maybe confirm that you actually have to give your flooring a little larger gap than 3/8" at each end. Jump to step #4.

Here is an example of a room I used this method in that had zero gap on one side.
- ○ Opposite wall measurement: 1/2"
- ○ Divided by two: 1/4"

So I assumed the original installer left about a 1/4" gap around the perimeter when the flooring was first installed. I needed to take off another 1/8" from each end of the flooring to make sure it at least had the recommended 3/8" gap.

Step 3) If you did not find any gaps around the entire perimeter? Then we will need to take off 3/8" around the entire room to allow for the correct expansion gap.

Step 4) There are a couple of ways to cut a laminate flooring around a perimeter with it still installed on the floor. We really don't want to have to pull planks up, and then cut them, because this could be a real pain. And nothing that we want to get into at this point. So, we will stick with cutting an expansion gap in the floor with it still installed. Here are a couple of options to do it.

4,A: Hammer and chisel: Yes, old-school! But a lot of installers prefer to use a simple hammer and chisel to cut a space in the flooring. This usually works well if you only need to remove a small amount of laminate flooring from an area in a room.

4,B: Saw Option: I personally use a mini circular saw to cut around the edge of a room. And the reason I purchased one of these saws was because of the smaller size, and you can get much closer to the wall with the blade to make the cuts needed.

To make a cut with a mini circular saw just make sure you set the depth right on the blade. You want to make sure it's set deep enough to cut the plank, but not go too deep into the subfloor! Of course, you will be cutting through some of the underlayment as well, but this won't be too much of a major problem. The best way to make sure you have the right depth is to grab a cut piece of the laminate, and then adjust the saw blade with the laminate held up right next to it.

Setting the correct cutting depth.

With the blade depth set, we can start to cut the laminate flooring around the perimeter. You should already know what you have to chop off from the first two steps we completed earlier.

You should start to cut right next to the wall, and use that as a guide to cut down the entire side of that room, or just the area you need to trim back. You may not be able to get exactly the measurement you need to cut off, because the blade may not allow you to get that close to the wall. But if you are using a mini circular saw, you should at least be able to get within a few sixteenths of an inch of your target measurement. Don't worry if you have to take off a little more than you really need, because when you put the moulding back on, it will hide the extra space. You will also find that when using a circular saw, because of the nature of the circular blade, you cannot get right into the corners to cut. For this area just grab a hammer and chisel to do the rest.

When you have completed your repair, just clean up the mess and then put the moulding back on and you are done! Safe in the knowledge that your problem will not return again.

If you cannot remove the moulding to complete this repair, and instead have to leave the moulding on to do it? Follow the same steps as above. But remember that you will have to buy an extra quarter-round moulding to hide the gap you just cut out. Take a look at the Moulding & Transitions chapter for pictures.

Other Tools You Can Use:
If you do not have a mini saw, you can use a Dremel, or Roto-zip, which I've seen done many times. Just make sure you get the right blades. Another

alternative is to use the hammer and chisel all the way around the room. But whatever you use, make sure you try it on a waste piece of laminate first, just so you can find out before you start that it can do the job.

Doctor Laminate - Replacing A Plank

I get it! Uncle Albert comes over, gets drunk, and then proceeds to show his former-glory feats of strength by dropping a heavy dumbbell right on your laminate flooring! It's a disaster! And no amount of filler or putty will save the floor now!

Things like this happen. So I thought I'd add a little section on how to replace a plank in the middle of the floor. But you can use this method for any damaged planks.

Uh Oh! We have a problem!

Things Needed

○   **Circular Saw**

○   **Sharpie Marker or Pen**

○   **Laminate Glue**

Step #1) On the damaged plank measure about 1 1/2" from each of the top corners inward, and make a dot. Then make a line with a marker or pen joining the outside corners to the dots.

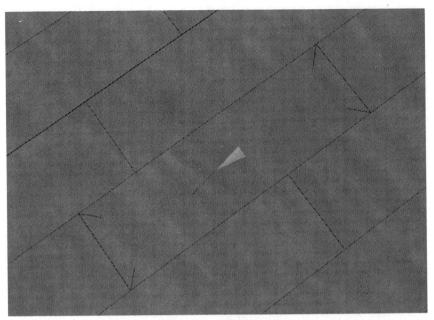

Drawing four lines 1 1/2" in from each corner.

Step #2) Grab a straight-edge or something that will give you a nice straight line and join all the inner dots together, to make this inner rectangle.

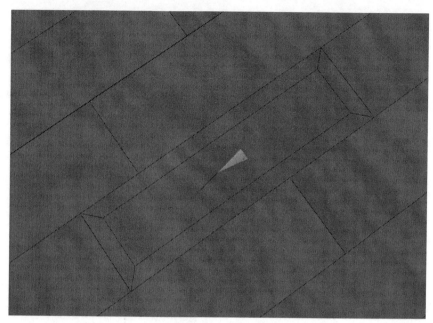

Use a sharpie or pen to connect the dots to make an inner rectangle.

Step #3) Cut out the inner rectangle using a saw with the correct depth setting. Then remove it.

Setting the cutting depth using a scrap piece of laminate flooring.

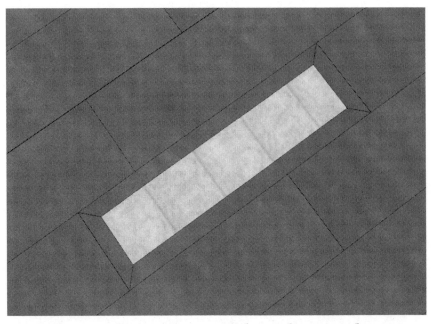

Cut out the inner rectangle with a circular saw and remove.

Step #4) Cut the small lines that run from the inner dots back to the outside corners. You will have to cut toward the other surrounding undamaged planks, so be really careful here and try not to cut into the other planks.

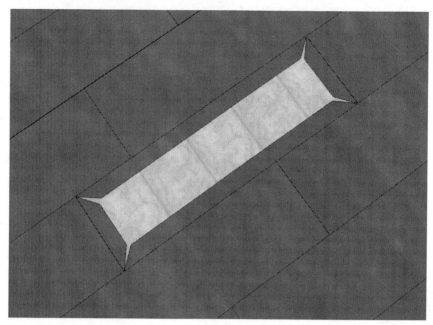

Cut the lines you made from each corner of the plank.

Step #5) Now just pull up and out on the remaining pieces of the plank. They should come out pretty easy, but if not cut a little more until you get right into the corner. Be pretty gentle when pulling out the damaged plank, because we want to keep the tongue and groove edges on the other planks surrounding it, fully in-tact.

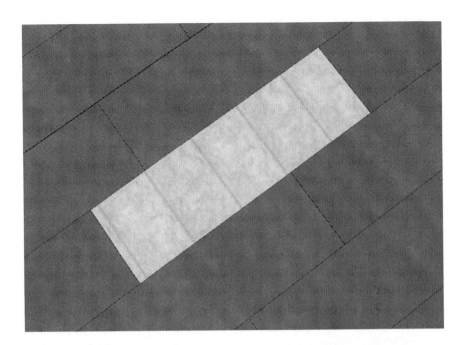

Step #6) With the entire plank removed, grab a new full plank and just trim off the two grooved edges, and only the tongue from the short end, leaving the long side of the plank with its tongue still there. Remember to only cut off the tongue and groove only, and not any of the top of the laminate board.

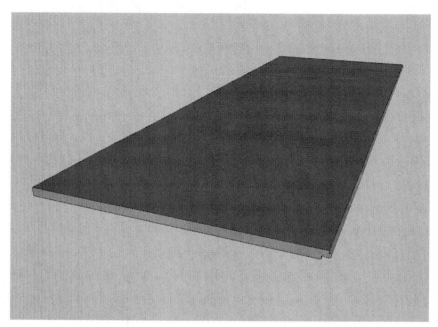

Edges trimmed, apart from the remaining long side tongue.

Step #7) Take your laminate glue and lightly squeeze it on the three sides of the board that have already been trimmed. We do not want to put any glue on the remaining tongue on this plank, because this is what we will be inserting into the planks on the floor. Don't go too heavy with the glue otherwise it will make a big mess when we lay down the new plank.

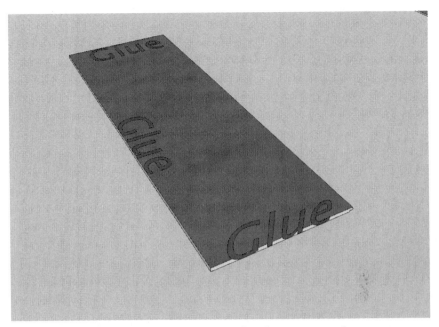

Glue each of the trimmed edges. But do not put any on the tongue edge

Step #8) Insert the tongue on the new plank into the unglued groove of the plank on the floor, and click it into place. When it's fully pressed down the glued edges will meet the sides of the other planks on the floor. If you get any glue on top of the planks, clean it up right away with a damp rag.

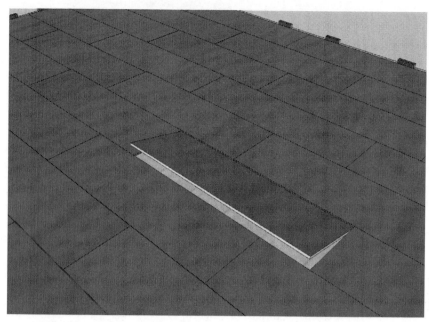

Placing the new plank into position. Fitting the tongue side into the groove of the neighboring planks.

Step #9) With the new plank in place, add something to weigh it down to set overnight and for at least 24 hours before you walk on it. I usually put a weight on a couple of the seams so everything remains level, even while it sets.

**Adding some weight to the repaired plank
overnight.**

Step #10) After 24 hours, remove and inspect the
new plank.

Good job! You just completed what most installers feel is a hard project! And with that, this completes our Repairing A Plank chapter, and our Doctor Laminate section. And also brings us to the end of this guide.

Final Words

Well, it's been fun to take you along this journey! And I'm hoping you have a perfect laminate flooring installation completed. You should be very proud of yourself if you do.

Now you can use this guide as a reference to do many more laminate flooring installations, or maybe even start your own business?;-) But whatever you do from here, I do hope you really enjoy your new floor for many years to come.

Before I go, I just wanted to offer you a way to get in contact with me with any questions, comments, success stories, or anything related to this guide-book. So please feel free to email me at.

howtoinstalllaminateflooring@gmail.com

It will be great to get to know my readers.

P.S: Any pictures you have of your own installation that you did using this guide-book, would be great to receive! Maybe I'll even use them in another edition someday.

Take care everyone! And thank you once again for purchasing my book.

Best of luck!
Gary Johnson.

Made in the USA
San Bernardino, CA
16 June 2016